Two One-Act Plays

Toronto at Dreamer's Rock

and

Education is Our Right

Two One-Act Plays

Toronto at Dreamer's Rock

and

Education is Our Right

Drew Hayden Taylor

FIFTH
HOUSE

Published by Fifth House Ltd.
A Fitzhenry & Whiteside Company
195 Allstate Parkway
Markham, ON L3R 4T8
www.fifthhousepublishers.ca

Library and Archives Canada Cataloguing in Publication Data
Taylor, Drew, 1962-
Education is our right; and, Toronto at dreamer's rock
ISBN 978-1-89725-270-3
I. Title. II. Title: Toronto at dreamer's rock.
PS8589.A94E38 1990 C812'.54 C90-097142-8

Cover design: Daniel Choi
Interior design: Robert MacDonald, MediaClones, Inc.
Toronto Ontario, Banff Alberta
Cover image courtesy: iStockphoto

The publisher gratefully acknowledges the support of the Canada Council for the Arts and the Department of Canadian Heritage and the Ontario Arts Council. We acknowledge the financial support of the Government of Canada through the Canada Book Fund (CBF) for our publishing program.

Translation in Toronto at Dreamer's Rock by Anita Knott.

10 9

Printed in Canada by Copywell

Contents

Stories are memories
that must be shared with the Universe,
because if they aren't
the Universe becomes a much smaller place.

To my mother,
who is still waiting for me
to get a real job

Acknowledgments

There are many people who are responsible, directly and indirectly, for the production and publication of these two plays. First and foremost are the two gentlemen I hold responsible for my introduction to the theater world: Tomson Highway, who, with a simple phone call to me, made it possible to stick my big toe in the sea of theater, and of course Larry Lewis, who taught me to swim in that sea.

I would also like to thank the De-Ba-Jeh-Mu-Jig Theatre Group, Audrey, Scan, Jeffrey and the rest of that colorful motley crew. Without their support and assistance there would be nothing but blank pages in this book.

Also a special thank you goes out to Lenore Kee-shig-Tobias, who helped me with the Nanabush legend, and to Esther Jocko, who advised me on the meaning of the crow — two special story tellers, two special women.

I have Anita Knott, my Aunt, to thank for assisting me in the translation of English into Ojibway. And I thank Teresa Castonguay, who suggested I try and have my plays published. *Toronto At Dreamer's Rock* and *Education Is Our Right* would be gathering dust on my shelf if it wasn't for her.

And finally, an obvious thank you goes out to Charles Dickens, wherever he may be.

Toronto at Dreamer's Rock

Production Notes

Toronto At Dreamer's Rock premiered on the Sheshegwaning Reserve, Manitoulin Island, Ontario, on 3 October 1989; it was produced by De-Ba-Jeh-Mu-Jig Theatre Group, Wikwemikong Unceded Reserve, Manitoulin Island, under the direction of Larry Lewis. The cast was as follows:

Rusty	*Dwayne Manitowabi*
Keesic	*Jeff Eshkawkogan*
Michael	*Herbie Barnes*

Dreamer's Rock is a real place with real power. It's located beside a highway on the Birch Island Reserve, and many people still go there for guidance. Care should be taken in the depiction of such a sacred place.

Toronto At Dreamer's Rock was designed as theater-in-the-round. The set should be elevated to give the impression of height and so the cast can look over the audience into the distance. It should also be fairly small to give the impression of the top of a rock outcropping. With such a confined space, the action and interrelation of the characters is amplified. *Toronto At Dreamer's Rock* is a dialogue-oriented play with a limited amount of action, so this will help intensify the movement.

The language used during the opening and closing sections of the play is Odawa/Ojibway, the language indigenous to the area of Dreamer's Rock. The final paragraphs of the play have purposely been left ambiguous to allow the production company a chance to research and fashion their own closing prayer and song, depending on the area and the nation they belong to.

Translation: Anita Knott.

Cast of Characters
(in order of appearance)

Rusty   a boy from the present

Keesic   a boy from the past

Michael   a boy from the future

Location:
Dreamer's Rock, Whitefish River (Birch Island)
Reserve, Ontario.

Time:
A relative term in this play, but it opens on a lazy
Saturday afternoon during the summer of 1989.

The setting is the top of Dreamer's Rock, a large outcropping of rock overlooking a scenic valley. It is early evening and a gentle breeze blows across the Rock. Rusty, a 16-year-old boy, is making his long climb up the hill. He is listening to his Walkman, singing a heavy metal tune at the top of his lungs. At the summit at last, he turns off his Walkman, then walks over to a ledge. He puts one foot up on the ledge and leans on it, looking at the wondrous scenery.

RUSTY:

My home, my people, my beer store. *He takes a bottle of Labatts Blue from his knapsack.* As far as my eye can see ... nothing but the little birds and me. *Chuckles.* For all it's worth.

He lifts the beer but before he can drink, he hears a crow cawing nearby. He stops, momentarily surprised.

RUSTY:

Get your own, stupid crow. *He looks around, shrugs, then holds up his beer in a mock salute.* To Dreamer's Rock, the one place on Manitoulin you won't find beer bottles. *He empties the bottle; the crow is cawing, but Rusty ignores it.* Until now, that is.

Drumming begins, amid the cawing of the crow. Rusty begins to bounce on the rock, against his will.

RUSTY:

What the ... ?

Suddenly, he is on his feet, doing an elaborate and exhausting crow hop. This dance lasts for two full minutes. Finally, he collapses into the indentation in the rock, a place worn away by the generations of boys who have gone to the rock for their vision. He looks up at the sky, fighting for breath.

RUSTY:

So blue, the sky. I wish I was up there. Speaking of Blue, I think it's time for another one.

He reaches for another beer. The crow cries out.

RUSTY:

Hit the road, crow. Fly, hit the sky. Can't you crows understand English? Then try some Indian. Kiss my geed, you stupid crow.

He jumps to a ledge on the rock. On another ledge, behind Rusty, Keesic appears.

KEESIC:

Kiss my geed? Nikiknendaan endaming ojiid, wag-nen dash kina endman. [I know what a geed is, but what does the rest of it mean?]

Rusty whirls around startled and finds himself looking at Keesic, a boy about his age. Keesic is dressed in a buckskin breech, identical to the kind worn several hundred years ago. Rusty doesn't know if this is a practical joke or something truly weird. He doesn't say anything for a moment as he slowly circles Keesic, trying to figure out what is going on. Keesic points at Rusty's clothing with a puzzled expression.

KEESIC:

Zhaawshkwaande, wagnen waawaashkeshwi yaan eshaawshkwaandeg? [Blue? What kind of buckskin is blue?]

Keesic reaches out to touch Rusty.

RUSTY:

Hey man, you stay away from me!

Keesic suddenly recognizes that things have changed. He checks out the surrounding area.

KEESIC:

O'omaa, zhinaagwad chi-minaabdamaabaan, kaawiin shwiingego. Mitigoog nepaatshinoog. [This place, it looks like the Place of Dreams, yet it isn't. The trees are all wrong.]

He turns to Rusty for help.

Kaawiin naasaab ezhimkwendmaan. Kiin na, manidoo dazhazhebik? Kaawiin gdo-shinaagzisii manido? Aaniindi yaayaan? [It's not like I remember it. Are you a spirit of the Rock? You don't look like a spirit. Where am I?]

RUSTY:

This is wild. *Looks at beer.* What are they putting in this stuff these days?

KEESIC:

Kaawiin gnistotoosnoon. Gnoonshin enweyang. [I don't understand you. Speak in our language.]

RUSTY:

That sounds like Indian. English, man. Talk to me in English. Where did you come from? What's with the get-up?

As he says this, Rusty reaches up to touch Keesic's sleeve, but the moment contact is made, the magic happens. Keesic and Rusty are thrown to the ground, they roll and come up on their knees, stunned and surprised. Keesic shakes his head clear, then looks at his sleeve where Rusty touched him, then back at Rusty.

KEESIC:

What did you do to me? What are you doing on this sacred site?

Keesic has barely finished the sentences when he realizes that he has changed languages. His face registers the shock. Rusty is oblivious to Keesic's predicament, only aware of his own.

RUSTY:

Hey buddy, that was a nasty fall you took there. You okay?

Keesic jerks his head up at Rusty's voice, totally amazed but still confused.

KEESIC:

I understand ...

Keesic grabs his own throat, terrified at the words coming out. Timidly he tries again.

KEESIC:

This is not my language ...

Keesic freezes again. Rusty, by this point, is beginning to get concerned.

RUSTY:

Hey, you don't look so hot. Geez, don't get sick on me, people probably wouldn't like it if you threw up on Dreamer's Rock, bad for tourists.

Keesic, not believing or understanding the new language he is speaking, grabs his throat and struggles to talk his own language, but he has forgotten it. Rusty misinterprets the action as choking and quickly pulls out a beer and gives it to Keesic to drink.

RUSTY:

Here, drink this.

KEESIC:

Is it water?

RUSTY:

To my family it is. They'd shower in it if they could.

Keesic comes close to Rusty, and notices an aroma on Rusty's breath.

KEESIC:

Whatever it is, it makes you smell.

RUSTY:

What are you, a critic? You try climbing up this rock carrying a couple bottles and see how you smell.

KEESIC:

It's not sweat I smell, something deeper.

RUSTY:

Hey, don't knock it till you've tried it. Here. *Handing bottle to Keesic.* Take a swig.

Keesic is hesitant to take it.

RUSTY:

What are you, a wimp?

Keesic takes a big gulp. His face quickly registers distaste as he spits it out, handing the bottle back to Rusty quite quickly. Rusty is chuckling to himself.

RUSTY:

Funny, that's exactly how I reacted to my first sip.

KEESIC:

That is horrible, like the water in a swamp.

Rusty smells his beer, shrugs, then takes a drink.

RUSTY:

I guess it is an acquired taste. Be happy you're not trying a 50, that stuff will rot out your sinuses.

KEESIC:

You prefer that ... that ... liquid over water?

RUSTY:

I've never brushed my teeth in it but yeah, I like it.

Keesic reaches over and touches Rusty's denim jacket with wonder.

KEESIC:

And this? What animal does this skin come from?

RUSTY:

Shrugging. It's a Levi.

KEESIC:

It looks like all one skin. This Levi must be a big animal. I am called Keesic.

RUSTY:

Keesic, eh? Your parents were born-again Indians too, huh? My middle name is Mukwa. That means bear.

KEESIC:

You must be a strong person to carry such a strong name.

RUSTY:

Proudly. Can bench 110 pounds.

KEESIC:

Bench? Pounds? You pound benches 110 times?

RUSTY:

Getting tired of the charade. Get out of town. Look, I was here first. I came up here to be alone for a while, if you don't mind.

KEESIC:

This is the Place of Dreams, you can never be alone here.

RUSTY:

> Well, not with people like you around, that's for
> sure. And what's with the fortune-cookie talk?
> You eat in a lot of Chinese restaurants or some-
> thing?

> *Rusty turns away and walks a bit, hoping Keesic
> will take the hint and disappear. Instead, Keesic
> seems to be thinking.*

KEESIC:

> It's been a while since I have eaten, but I don't
> think I've ever hunted a *Struggling with the word.*
> Chinese restaurant.

RUSTY:

> Very funny.

KEESIC:

> It is summer now. *He looks around.* I've just
> spent the last three days fighting the wind and the
> snow to get here. And only to be met by summer.
> Why?

RUSTY:

> Maybe to wear one of those white jackets with the
> long arms that wrap right around ...

KEESIC:

> Mukwa, do you know why ...

> *Rusty answers quickly and harshly.*

RUSTY:

> Mukwa? Hold it right there, Tonto, people call me
> Rusty around here. And don't tell anybody I told
> you my middle name. It's embarrassing.

KEESIC:

Rusty? What kind of name is Rusty?

RUSTY:

Confused. What do you mean what kind of name? It's a name, my name. You got a problem with it, buddy?

KEESIC:

No, it's just that I have never heard of anything or anyone called a "Rusty."

RUSTY:

When I was young, my hair was kinda red, sort of a rust color, so I got called Rusty. Happy?

KEESIC:

But what is a rust?

RUSTY:

You've been out in the woods too long. Rust, you know, when metal gets old and wet, it turns rusty and falls apart. It, like, decays, I guess is the right word.

KEESIC:

Metal?

RUSTY:

You're really playing this to the hilt, aren't you? Metal, like bendable rock.

Keesic wanders away for a moment, perplexed, then turns to Rusty.

KEESIC:

You were named after rotting rocks?

RUSTY:

Insulted. My rocks ain't rotten. It's just a nick-name. It don't mean anything.

KEESIC:

But what power does a name have if it doesn't have a purpose or meaning?

Rusty, thinking his name is being insulted again, begins to get angry.

RUSTY:

Okay, I've had enough of this. If you don't like my name then just say it to my face then. Well, you got something to say?

KEESIC:

Backing off. No, it's your name. I'm sure it's a fine name. Rusty.

RUSTY:

Yeah, well watch it next time.

KEESIC:

To himself. Strange people, what happened to the naming, in this strange place? I don't know where I am.

RUSTY:

It ain't Kansas.

KEESIC:

I must know, is this the Place of Dreams?

RUSTY:

> Of course, it's Dreamer's Rock. Everybody knows that.

KEESIC:

> Dreamer's Rock? I must be in the Land of Spirits. But why would the Great Spirit bring me here?

RUSTY:

> What are you talking about?

KEESIC:

> *Ignoring Rusty, thinking.* The last thing I remember, before seeing you, was climbing up this place you call Dreamer's Rock. The rock was coated with snow and ice. My fingers bled from holding on, but I was finally here.

> *Rusty is waiting to hear the rest of the story.*

RUSTY:

> And?

KEESIC:

> And what?

RUSTY:

> What happened next?

KEESIC:

> *Shrugging.* I slipped.

RUSTY:

> You slipped!

KEESIC:

The rock was covered with ice ... I went head over foot to the bottom and ended up here.

RUSTY:

Not believing. At the top?

KEESIC:

Keesic rubs his head painfully. Some time the Creator works in mysterious ways.

RUSTY:

I guess so.

KEESIC:

Pointing. That mountain. That was never here.

RUSTY:

Looking. That ain't no mountain, it's a cement factory.

KEESIC:

Cement factory? What's that?

By this point, Rusty is beginning to get a little exasperated.

RUSTY:

It's a place that makes cement, you idiot.

KEESIC:

Cement?

RUSTY:

Yeah, like man-made rock, you know.

KEESIC:

Why would man want to make rock? *Gestures toward the landscape.* There's rock as far as the eye can see.

RUSTY:

Yeah, but you can shape cement.

KEESIC:

Into what?

RUSTY:

Well ... a floor to stand on.

KEESIC:

Like this? *Points to the ground.* This already has a floor of rock.

RUSTY:

Getting frustrated. It's movable. You can put it places where there isn't a surface like this.

KEESIC:

Then this cement is lighter than rock?

RUSTY:

No!

KEESIC:

Then why ... ?

RUSTY:

Yelling. Never mind!

Keesic reacts to Rusty's frustration by backing up a bit.

KEESIC:

> Not so loud. You'd think I was down by the lake the way you yelled at me.

RUSTY:

> Okay, I'm sorry.

KEESIC:

> And those lines over there *Pointing.* cutting through the forest. What do you call them?

RUSTY:

> *Looking.* Oh. Those are roads.

KEESIC:

> Roads. And what do these roads do?

RUSTY:

> People drive on them. What else would you do with them?

KEESIC:

> I can't tell from here, what do they look like?

RUSTY:

> Roads? They are like very wide, hard paths, I guess.

KEESIC:

> Paths? That big? Hunting must be good to make people fat enough to need a path that wide. I have this picture in my mind of these roads bringing all these fat young boys here for their dreams.

RUSTY:

> You're talking about dream quests, aren't you? They don't do that much any more, it sort of died

out about a hundred years ago I think. Occasionally you hear of some crazy fool trying it, usually the kid of one of those fool drummer types, but not much.

Keesic looks startled, and a bit stunned.

KEESIC:

No more dreams, no more visions, no fasting? Why?

RUSTY:

I don't know. They just don't. None of my friends seem to want to sit out in the bush and starve for a week. Cuts into their social life.

Keesic kneels down at a particular spot, gently touching it, like he's remembering something. His voice takes on a gentle tone. Rusty is intrigued by Keesic. He's being drawn into his power.

KEESIC:

I think I am beginning to understand now. My visit to the Place of Dreams took place long before your time.

RUSTY:

Who are you? Rip Van McGregor? You can't be much older than me.

KEESIC:

I believe I am 16 winters old.

RUSTY:

I thought so. It's hard to pull something over on me when I've only had a couple beer.

KEESIC:

> But I am 16 winters when there are no roads or strange man-made mountains.

RUSTY:

> *Disbelieving.* Uh huh. Sure you were.

KEESIC:

> My vision told me nothing of this, any of this.

RUSTY:

> Your vision? You had a vision here? I don't remember hearing anything about that, and my mother's the biggest gossip around. She knows everything that goes on in the village.

KEESIC:

> I was here for five days with nothing but wind and the sun for companionship. I drank water, I chanted, I prayed for my vision to appear. Finally, one dark and windy night, it came. And went.

RUSTY:

> So that's how you got to be this crazy. No wonder. You were probably hallucinating or something with no food in five days.

KEESIC:

> The Creator told me how to live in images and stories that took time to figure out. But that is the way of the Creator. All things worth having must be earned.

RUSTY:

> So why are you up here again? Looking for DreamQuest, the sequel?

KEESIC:

> *Not listening.* My vision told me that I am to follow the path of medicine.

RUSTY:

> And the problem is?

KEESIC:

> Sadly. I can't do it. I'm not strong enough. I'm afraid I will embarrass my family and people if I fail.

RUSTY:

> Bad scene. So if all your troubles started here, why come back?

KEESIC:

> This place helped me once. I was hoping it could do it again. Even in winter this place called out to me, and I came. And here I sit now. With you.

RUSTY:

> In the land of roads and cement factories.

KEESIC:

> Yes, strange, is it not?

> *Rusty is silent before he gives a short chuckle.*

RUSTY:

> And in this so-called vision of yours, there were no little white people running around telling you to go home and stay out of trouble?

KEESIC:

> White people? Is that what was in your vision?

RUSTY:

I hate to bust your metaphysical bubble there, Moses, but I came here to drink. That's it in a nutshell. *Turns to grab his beer.* Speaking of nuts ...

Michael, dressed in unidentifiable futuristic garb, stands on the rock, staring at Keesic and Rusty.

MICHAEL:

I don't believe this.

Keesic and Rusty scream aloud, and freeze in their tracks.

KEESIC:

Yiiii!

RUSTY:

Holy ...

MICHAEL:

They sound authentic.

Michael walks up to them and examines them closely, beginning with Keesic.

MICHAEL:

Pre-contact, no doubt. I'd say late woodland period. *Touching Rusty's jacket.* Standard outfitting for the 20th-century aboriginal. Denim. Once referred to as "jean."

KEESIC:

Feeling Michael's sleeve. Another strange animal.

MICHAEL:

Almost distastefully. Not animal, synthetic.

RUSTY:

Where are you people coming from?

KEESIC:

I am called Keesic, strange one. Are you from this time, too?

MICHAEL:

Do I look like it?

KEESIC:

No. You look funny. Funnier than this one.

MICHAEL:

Where I come from, today is the first of May, 2095. *He sees something in the distance.* That, that's an *Struggling with the word.* automobile, isn't it? Almost looks like a '93 Eclipse.

RUSTY:

A '93 what?

MICHAEL:

I'm being rude. *To Keesic, enunciating very clearly.* I am Michael. *Touching his heart with his fist. He turns to Rusty, extending his hand.* I believe the contemporary greeting is "I'm pleased to meet you, and you might be?"

RUSTY:

Voice cracking. Rusty.

The name seems to have struck a chord. Michael studies Rusty's face.

RUSTY:

What are you lookin' at?

MICHAEL:

Rusty what?

RUSTY:

Just Rusty to you, pal. Why?

MICHAEL:

You look very familiar.

RUSTY:

Snickers. Maybe you're my great-great-great-grandson. That's a laugh.

MICHAEL:

I know your face from somewhere, and your name. Rusty! Rusty!

RUSTY:

So if you're from the future, I'd have to be famous for a hundred years or something for you to know me. *It dawns on him.* Famous! Am I famous, huh, am I? What did I do? Am I a movie star or something? A rock star? *He stops.* What am I saying? My God, it's contagious. I'm crazy too.

KEESIC:

You are from this one's future?

MICHAEL:

I didn't think it was possible.

KEESIC:

All things are possible here.

This is too much for Rusty. He starts backing up and almost falls off the rock. He looks at the others as if they are crazy.

RUSTY:

What is this? You guys travel in pairs or something? Who are you?

MICHAEL:

Philosophically, psychologically, economically, culturally? Be specific.

RUSTY:

Yelling. Who the hell are you?

MICHAEL:

You look upset.

KEESIC:

He yells a lot.

RUSTY:

Turns to Keesic. You shut up, I still haven't figured you out yet. Look, I don't know where you guys are coming from, but I want you to go back there now. I mean it.

Michael turns to Keesic, ignoring Rusty.

MICHAEL:

This is interesting. Judging by the material and stitching pattern, I'd hazard a guess of approximately 500 years ago my time. I knew it was pre-contact.

KEESIC:

Pre-contact.

Rusty throws his hands up in frustration and turns away.

RUSTY:

And he still has all his teeth.

MICHAEL:

It means you were here before the white man was, totally untouched, pure. I have a history teacher that would love a chance to interview subject matter like you. Both of you, actually.

Rusty steps in between the two, separating them, and then turns to Michael.

RUSTY:

Wait a minute, just wait a minute, Flash Gordon, I'm tired of having my leg pulled. It's probably halfway down the hill by now. And I don't buy this time thing either. For the last time, who are you? Buckskin Bill here won't give me a straight answer. You got one? Is this a regular thing with you guys, or what?

Michael walks around Rusty and looks off in the distance, taking a deep breath. Keesic looks puzzled.

KEESIC:

How do you manage to hunt and feed your family when you talk so much and so loudly?

RUSTY:

> I think I'm getting one of my mother's headaches. I never should have come up here.

KEESIC:

> I've been to the Place of Dreams many times, but never like this. Michael, I am called Keesic. Welcome.

MICHAEL:

> *Animated.* I have this pet theory about this particular spot.

Rusty makes a rude noise.

MICHAEL:

> Of course, I'm the only one who believes it, but I think it's true. Over those thousands of years that boys had their vision quests here, this area amassed a tremendous reservoir of power. And probably in the time between the two of you this power has gone largely unused. It's a type of emotional power, similar to the Poltergeist phenomenon common in Germany, and Rusty must have triggered it somehow! This is a pretty powerful place, Rusty, even in my time.

RUSTY:

> I don't care about this place, I just want to find out where you people are popping out of and why. Who's next, the ghost of Christmas present?

Michael bursts out laughing, but Keesic doesn't understand it.

MICHAEL:
> Don't worry, Rusty, I'm fairly certain I'm not a ghost. How about you, Keesic?

But Keesic has no idea what is going on.

KEESIC:
> Ghost? What?

RUSTY:
> This is one of those days I should have gotten up, eaten my Rice Crispies, and gone right back to bed again. Look guys, I just wanted a nice quiet beer, and I didn't even get that with that damn crow bugging the hell out of me.

Suddenly Rusty has Keesic's complete attention.

KEESIC:
> Crow?! Did you say you heard a crow? What did it say?

RUSTY:
> Caw. What else does a crow say? It just screeched a few times when I drank my beer, then it went away. *Keesic looks worried.* Why? What does a crow have to do with anything?

KEESIC:
> I don't know. But you know what a crow is.

Michael and Rusty, confused, look at each other.

RUSTY:
> *Bluffing.* Yeah, of course I do, but you better explain it to Michael anyways.

KEESIC:

> They are the messengers of the Creator and other powerful beings. If that crow was talking to you, it must have been for a reason. You should learn to listen, Rusty, it might have been trying to tell you something important.

RUSTY:

> Like where the garbage dump is.

MICHAEL:

> Messengers of the Creator! How quaint!

RUSTY:

> Forget the stupid crow. If everything you two are telling me is true, then why me, why you, why here, why now? *Pause.* I don't believe this. And why am I still talking to you? My mother warned me about people like you but she said they all lived in Toronto.

KEESIC:

> Toronto?!

RUSTY:

> You know about Toronto? Then you aren't real.

KEESIC:

> I'm as real as you are. My people are great traders. We make trips to the south for goods. And in trade it is better to understand the language of the people you are dealing with. Those people to the south have a word for where people gather to trade, but it covers any place where important things happen. It's called "Toronto."

RUSTY:

So we're like a little mini-Toronto right up here. That's cool.

MICHAEL:

Actually in my time, the metropolis of Toronto almost reaches to the shore of Huron. Traders, eh? What nation are you, anyways?

Keesic looks perplexed.

KEESIC:

We are the people.

MICHAEL:

Did other nations have a name for you?

KEESIC:

We are known by some tribes as Odawa.

Rusty's ears perk up at that word.

RUSTY:

Hey, wow. I'm half Odawa. This is bizarre.

KEESIC:

Half Odawa? What is your other half?

RUSTY:

Ojibway, and I think there's supposed to be some Pottawatami floating around in my blood somewhere, too.

MICHAEL:

Genealogically, I am mostly Odawa.

KEESIC:

> Ojibway? They live far to the northwest. And the Pottawatami don't live near here. How does their blood flow in your veins?

RUSTY:

> It's the Three Fires.

KEESIC:

> I don't understand.

RUSTY:

> You don't understand the Three Fires? What kind of Indian are you anyways?

MICHAEL:

> *Stepping between them.* A lot of nations were displaced by the coming of the whiteman. And, as a result, traditional migratory patterns were disrupted. Eventually, the Ojibway, Odawa, and Pottawatami reached an agreement whereby they would share Manitoulin Island.

KEESIC:

> That's the third time you've mentioned this white man. Why is he white? Is he not well?

RUSTY:

> Well, that's a judgment call.

MICHAEL:

> I guess you could say he is another nation far to the east in your time. And in time, he came to this island here.

KEESIC:

> I have heard stories about these people. But I thought they were just stories.

Michael shakes his head confidently.

MICHAEL:

> Well, they're coming. Taking an educated guess, I would estimate you to be from approximately the 1590s. And Champlain landed in this area around 1615. We're talking a couple of decades at the most.

RUSTY:

> *Laughing.* Boy, do you have a surprise coming. Guess who's coming to dinner? You better put out an extra 250 million plates, but be sure and check the silverware after.

Even Michael laughs at that one. But Keesic remains in the dark. Michael picks up Rusty's bottle of beer and examines it as if it were an interesting museum piece.

MICHAEL:

> Labatts Blue! I didn't know they made this way back then ... I mean now.

KEESIC:

> I don't like it.

MICHAEL:

> Neither did I. *An idea occurs.* That's it, maybe that's why we were brought here! *Keesic and Michael look at each other.* To defend Dreamer's Rock.

KEESIC:
> Against what?

MICHAEL:
> *Holds up beer bottle.* This!

KEESIC:
> That!

> *Rusty grabs the bottle and puts it in his pack.*

RUSTY:
> It's an empty beer bottle. What's there to defend?

MICHAEL:
> This particular period of time was known in Aboriginal history as the "Alcoholic Era." From the mid 1800s till the late 1900s, Native people suffered due to an addiction to this liquid. Of course, the problem didn't start and stop at those times. It slowly led up to it then tapered off, much the same way the Black Plague did in medieval Europe.

KEESIC:
> Worse than swamp water.

RUSTY:
> Alcoholic Era? Black plague? I'm just having a beer, not starting an epidemic.

MICHAEL:
> When's the last time you consumed enough of this liquid to reach your desired effect?

RUSTY:

You mean get drunk? Last weekend I guess.

MICHAEL:

I thought so.

RUSTY:

Don't give me that holier-than-thou attitude. You mean to tell me that there is no such thing as beer in the future?

MICHAEL:

Of course there is, but people don't die from it any more. Two hundred years of suicide is enough.

Rusty shakes his head as he tries to figure Michael out.

RUSTY:

How old are you?

MICHAEL:

Sixteen. Why?

RUSTY:

You sure don't act or talk like you're 16.

MICHAEL:

Oh trust me, I am 16, but I study history. You know what they say, "Those who don't remember the past are condemned to relive it."

KEESIC:

But what if it is a good past?

MICHAEL:
>   What?

KEESIC:
>   What if the past you are remembering is a good
>   one? Shouldn't you relive it?

Michael is stumped.

MICHAEL:
>   Um ...

RUSTY:
>   Ah, this is crazy. *To Keesic.* I thought you were
>   bad, he's worse.

KEESIC:
>   Rusty, why is this smelly water you drink so
>   important to you?

RUSTY:
>   *Really losing his temper.* It's a beer, not some
>   stupid philosophy, there's nothing to understand.
>   Why is it so hard for you to believe that?

KEESIC:
>   Rusty, why are you so angry all the time?

MICHAEL:
>   All this frustration and aggression. Why?

Rusty almost explodes with frustration.

RUSTY:
>   Ah, damn, damn, damn, damn, damn.

KEESIC:

Nice. Could almost be a chant.

MICHAEL:

To some people I think it is.

Keesic kneels down beside Rusty.

KEESIC:

One time when I was young, I don't think I'd seen a dozen winters yet ...

MICHAEL:

Traditional Native Storytelling! *He sits, cross-legged, in happy anticipation.* Please, proceed.

Keesic eyes him narrowly before continuing.

KEESIC:

I was gathering bird eggs for my mother. I came across this duck that was splashing around in the water like it had a broken wing. I love duck, so I went after it, but every time I got close it would splash farther away. I followed that duck halfway across the lake before it miraculously healed and flew away. I told my father about this, and he laughed.

RUSTY:

And the point is?

Michael has his arm up, begging to answer the question. He can't restrain himself.

MICHAEL:

Don't you see?! The duck was protecting its eggs,

something very delicate and precious to it. It lured
Keesic away, a long futile chase to divert his
attention. People do the same thing sometimes
without knowing it.

RUSTY:

I'm trying to save my eggs?

MICHAEL:

There is something in you that you are protecting
with this anger. You are just using it to divert
people's attention.

RUSTY:

Quack quack.

MICHAEL:

What are you afraid of?

RUSTY:

I'm not afraid of anything, you idiot.

MICHAEL:

Confused and disappointed. Touchy. I always
read that adolescence in this time was supposed to
be a time of fun. Drive-in movies, hula hoop, Bay
City Rollers. *Singing.* S-A-T-U-R-D-A-Y NIGHT!

RUSTY:

Bay City Rollers!? Give me a break. You don't
know my life, so don't start giving me suggestions
on how to run it. Until you've lived my life and
felt what I feel, stay off my back.

KEESIC:

I don't think you like your life.

RUSTY:

Hey, it's the only one I got.

MICHAEL:

But is it the one you want?

RUSTY:

Do I got a choice? Does it really matter? Okay, I can't go to Hawaii. I'll never own a Porsche, I'll never have all those things I see on television. I'm lucky if I get a new pair of jeans for the first day of school. What's there to be happy for? I'm terrible in school, so I can't walk that side of the tracks, and as for going the traditional Indian route, that's even worse. I hate cleaning fish and I'm a terrible hunter. I don't fit in here. Last year my father took me hunting, I shot my own dog. I can't do any-thing right except drink. You wanted to know my problems, there they are. I hope you enjoy them.

Everybody is silent for a moment, letting the emotion sink in.

MICHAEL:

So that's how you deal with your problems. I must say that I'm not particularly impressed. But here. Have another beer! Everybody has problems, but they cope with them.

RUSTY:

Oh yeah? Look at you. I have no idea what kind of outfit that is but it don't look like you're too bad off. And judging by the way you talk and the things you've said, you're doing great in school and you know a lot of things. Keesic here only has to worry about hunting enough to eat. They didn't have complicated problems back then. At least you both have your own worlds to fit in and return to. I'm stuck smack-dab in the middle of a family war, between one uncle that's called "Closer" because they say he's closed every bar in Ontario, and my other Uncle Stan, who is basically a powwow Indian, I never know what's going on. Sometimes I don't know if I should go into a sweatlodge or a liquor store. Sometimes they tear me apart. I don't fit in. Like tonight. It's Saturday and what am I doing? Standing on a rock, out in the middle of the woods, talking to two people who probably don't exist. How's that for a social life? Instead of looking at the two of you, I should be out with some hot babe. *To himself.* I should have asked her out. I should have.

MICHAEL:

Asked who out?

RUSTY:

There's a girl I kinda like in town. For all the good it does me.

MICHAEL:

What do you mean?

RUSTY:

The girl doesn't know I exist. I don't know if it's because I'm Indian or because she thinks I'm a flake. I'm not sure which is worse.

KEESIC:

Looking puzzled. What's an Indian?

Both Rusty and Michael look at Keesic.

RUSTY:

Oh, that's right, you've never heard the word.

MICHAEL:

It's a generic term used to describe all original inhabitants of this land. It was popular up until approximately 100 years ago, my time. In fact, right around your time. *Points to Rusty.* The more politically correct term in this day and age are "Native" or "Aboriginal."

KEESIC:

So we are all ... Indian?

RUSTY:

Yup.

KEESIC:

Why would an Indian girl not like you for being Indian?

RUSTY:

She's not.

KEESIC:

She's one of these white people?

RUSTY:

Uh huh.

KEESIC:

Interesting. What does she look like?

RUSTY:

Her name is Sherry. Doesn't that sound great? Oh, she's real pretty. She's got long blonde hair ...

KEESIC:

Blonde?

RUSTY:

Yellow.

Rusty, feeling more at ease, is exploding with energy. He does a hand spring to shake himself out of it.

KEESIC:

White people got yellow hair? Just like the sun?

RUSTY:

Smiling. And twice as hot.

Rusty begins moving along the edge of the rock, balancing himself. It's a sort of game with him, one that Keesic and Michael join in. Michael has no talent for this, however, and is rather slow.

KEESIC:

During the summer, when my family joins other families to hunt and fish, there's always this girl that would be at the camp. Her name is Nungohns. For the past few summer now, we've watched each other, always from a distance. We talk, but that's about it.

RUSTY:

So what's the problem? Just date the girl. You make it sound like it's a terrible thing. What's the matter? Her parents don't like you?

KEESIC:

We are of the same clan.

RUSTY:

> That's like being in the same family, isn't it?

KEESIC:

> Families are recognized by what clan they belong to. They represent a particular family grouping, and you are not allowed to hunt or eat the flesh of your clan animal. And you cannot marry someone from your clan.

MICHAEL:

> Are you related to her?

KEESIC:

> Many generations ago, but we might as well be total strangers for all that it matters.

RUSTY:

> No way of getting around it?

KEESIC:

> It is not permitted.

MICHAEL:

> Maybe you and this Mongoose could elope.

KEESIC AND RUSTY:

> Nungohns!

MICHAEL:

> Sorry.

KEESIC:

> If I could turn our backs on our family's ways, where would we go? I don't know about here, but where I come from, two people alone in the bush

may survive the summer, but not the winter. Not
when you no longer exist in the village's eyes.
What if something bad happens, who do you go to
for help? That's the way it is.

*All three are lying back on the rock, legs dangling
over the edge.*

RUSTY:

Well, at least your girl likes you. As for mine, I
might as well be a doorknob.

MICHAEL:

Where do you know this girl from?

RUSTY:

School, where else? It's one of the only reasons I go
any more.

MICHAEL:

Obviously you don't like school.

RUSTY:

Nothing gets past you, Sherlock. It's just that I
have a problem trying to figure out why I should
care when Napoleon became emperor of France.

MICHAEL:

1799, I believe.

KEESIC:

Who is Napoleon?

RUSTY:

Some French guy.

KEESIC:
> What's a French guy?

MICHAEL:
> All knowledge matters. In order for the mind to grow it must consume a variety of subjects. Your mind is just like your body, if you only eat one type of food, you die.

RUSTY:
> My mother's been living on Kraft Dinner for the past 10 years and she's still kicking.

MICHAEL:
> Oh, be serious!

KEESIC:
> Will Rusty ever need this knowledge of Nap ... Nap ...

RUSTY:
> Napoleon.

KEESIC:
> Napoleon.

MICHAEL:
> Granted he may never find a practical use for such knowledge, but it could influence other thoughts he may have.

RUSTY:
> I like being *Stressing the joke.* under the influence. Ah, screw Napoleon, hey, Obi-Michael Kenobi, you got girl or school problems where you come from?

MICHAEL:

I have what could be referred to as a girlfriend. So far anyways.

RUSTY:

That don't sound good.

MICHAEL:

It isn't. She's not impressed with my preoccupation with the past. She'd rather I be more pragmatic and less, less ... what's the word ... less airy, theoretical, esoteric ... I hestitate to use the word "spiritual."

RUSTY:

Geez, you use a lot of big words.

MICHAEL:

It's important to be accurate.

RUSTY:

Sounds like you got money and power. I wish I had your problems. You want to stay here while I go back to your place?

MICHAEL:

Sadly. What do they say in this time, it ain't all peachy keen. We've lost our culture. It really isn't there. It's all been explained away or forgotten or just walked away from. Even our cheekbones are going. The poverty that once plagued us is gone, but at what cost? The language only exists on digital discs, the sweatlodge is gone, and Dreamer's Rock is a tourist attraction.

KEESIC:

How can so much be lost?

RUSTY:

I don't know.

MICHAEL:

I used to come here when I was a kid. I still do. *He pulls some sweetgrass from his pocket.* I'm the only one on the reserve who has any sweetgrass, and I think I'm the only one who knows how to find it.

RUSTY:

Where did you get it?

MICHAEL:

In the field that overlooks the island in the bay. It's the only place left on the reserve.

RUSTY:

Hey, I know that place. I used to pick sweetgrass there with my aunt. You can smell it 10 minutes before you get there.

MICHAEL:

That hasn't changed.

RUSTY:

Smells good.

MICHAEL:

There are plans to turn the field into a helipad.

RUSTY:

That's bizarre. Well, maybe I can leave you a little time capsule there.

MICHAEL:

You did!

RUSTY:

I did?

MICHAEL:

Two years ago, I found a capsule protruding from the ground. In it I found some material addressed to me, dated 2023. Needless to say I was greatly surprised.

RUSTY:

And I left it? In 2023? What did I leave?

MICHAEL:

Something very interesting. It was sort of responsible for igniting my interest in the past.

Keesic takes the sweetgrass, examines it, and smells it.

KEESIC:

This is the first sweetgrass you've picked?

MICHAEL:

No, but it always ends up the same, falling apart into a mess.

KEESIC:

You don't braid it?

MICHAEL:

I have a problem with tactile maneuvering.

Keesic starts to braid the sweetgrass. Rusty intrudes rudely.

RUSTY:

> To heck with your tactical maneuvers and your sweetgrass. Cough it up, buddy. What did I leave in that there time capsule?

MICHAEL:

> Just some material, that's all.

RUSTY:

> No, no, no, no, no. You said "something very interesting." What is "something very interesting," Michael?

MICHAEL:

> I don't think I should tell you.

RUSTY:

> Well I do. If I left it, it's my property.

MICHAEL:

> In 2023?

RUSTY:

> That's beside the point.

MICHAEL:

> No, that is the point. Then I think you were ready to leave it, ready to share it.

RUSTY:

> *Frustrated.* "It." What is "it"?

MICHAEL:

> You're getting angry again.

Keesic looks up from his sweetgrass braiding.

KEESIC:

See how you are?

Rusty growls.

MICHAEL:

If I tell you the future, your future, it may change things.

RUSTY:

Too late. I know about you, don't I? What's the difference with this?

MICHAEL:

This information will affect your life, maybe negatively in this crucial and formative stage. I don't think it's advisable at the moment.

Rusty nearly strangles Michael.

RUSTY:

You think you're hot stuff, huh? Give a guy a little information and he starts wanting to play government, telling you only what he thinks you need to know. If you're so smart, go check out that hollow in 2095. I'll leave you another time capsule there.

Keesic looks over the cliff.

KEESIC:

That's poison ivy.

RUSTY:

Yeah, and I'll bet he's just itching to find out the significance of that, huh?

MICHAEL:

I don't believe you're the same Rusty.

RUSTY:

As what, Buck Rogers?

MICHAEL:

The wit is still there, but not the control. Until you find some control, I don't think you're ready for the future.

RUSTY:

Fine. You keep your future. I'll find out mine soon enough, in 30 years.

MICHAEL:

Thirty-four.

RUSTY:

Whatever.

MICHAEL:

It's best to be precise.

RUSTY:

Look, I don't need your information and I don't want it.

Michael approaches him, about to say something.

RUSTY:

Stop! Don't even mention the subject to me again. Even if you begged me to let you tell me every-thing you know, I wouldn't even listen. Jerk!

Rusty jumps to another, isolated place on the rock and pouts. By this time, Keesic has braided the sweetgrass and now offers it to Michael.

MICHAEL:
Touched. Thank you.

KEESIC:
Have you ever used it to smudge?

MICHAEL:
I know it's to purify yourself, but other than that, I don't know how.

KEESIC:
No language. No dream quests. No rituals. Isn't there anything left? Warriors!

RUSTY:
Sorry, but there are no more warriors.

KEESIC:
No warriors? No battles? What about the Nodwheg? Surely you must fight them.

MICHAEL:
The what?

RUSTY:
Iroquois. Mohawk, to be exact. No, we're friends with them now.

KEESIC:
Horrified. With the Nodwheg? No!

RUSTY:

Sorry to tell you this, buddy, but I was at a baseball tournament of theirs just a few weeks ago.

KEESIC:

If there are no more warriors, how does a young man get honor?

RUSTY:

Honor means different things to different people. My uncle says the most honorable thing he ever did was marry my aunt.

KEESIC:

But what about bravery?

RUSTY:

You ever met my aunt?

KEESIC:

So much is different. Do we still eat food?

RUSTY:

Are you kidding? I don't have an uncle under 250 pounds or an aunt under 200. Does that answer your question?

KEESIC:

Good. It's nice to know that hasn't changed.

Keesic rubs his stomach. Mentioning food has made him remember his hunger.

MICHAEL:

Are you hungry?

KEESIC:

> I haven't eaten much in the last three days. Winters can be hard, and so can hunger. I wish I had some muskrat. That's my favorite food.

MICHAEL:

> I could never understand the fascination of eating the flesh of animals that come from a swamp. I find it disgusting.

RUSTY:

> Be nice. I'm kinda partial to moose. Especially moose burgers.

KEESIC:

> My father would always let me have the first slice from a kill. I would always pray to the Great Spirit that his hunt would be successful. Then there's pheasant.

RUSTY:

> Mmmmmmmm.

KEESIC:

> Although many times we go hungry. Sometimes we drink only teas for days. The winters can be long.

RUSTY:

> Boy, I thought I had it hard. I've never really been hungry. The hardest thing I ever had to deal with was my father.

KEESIC:

> Your father?

RUSTY:

Yeah, he has a great backhand, and I don't mean tennis. One of the scariest times of my life was just after I turned 12. I found out I couldn't fit under the bed and had to find a new place to hide. Well, at least I can outrun him now.

KEESIC:

Your father hurt you? I don't understand. Why?

RUSTY:

I don't know. Go ask him.

KEESIC:

But children are a gift from the Creator. They are put here for a purpose.

RUSTY:

Yeah, well he had a purpose for me all right.

Keesic slaps Michael to get his attention.

KEESIC:

And you?

MICHAEL:

Not in my family, but yeah, it still exists in some places.

KEESIC:

The more I hear the more is lost.

MICHAEL:

Oh come on. It's not all that bad. Believe me. Look at me!

Keesic and Rusty laugh helplessly. Michael's feelings are a little hurt.

MICHAEL:

I lead a happy life. I'm graduating top of my class. No problems.

RUSTY:

I thought you said everybody's got problems?

MICHAEL:

I did, didn't I?

KEESIC:

So nothing is wrong in your world? Everything is fine? People don't hurt? Everybody is happy?

MICHAEL:

We're only allowed to swim one week a summer.

KEESIC:

One week a summer?

RUSTY:

You're kidding. Why?

MICHAEL:

That's when they purify the lake. It only lasts a week and then the water goes bad again. There's a new type of algae that thrives on ultraviolet rays and pollution. The lake is covered all summer long like a green blanket. But for the past three years there's been a festival on the island called Swimming Days. I envy the two of you. Being able to swim anywhere. Even drink the water. It must be wonderful.

RUSTY:

Gee, I never thought about it before.

KEESIC:

And you call this no problem?

MICHAEL:

It's called keeping things in perspective.

KEESIC:

Perspective. Perspective. I don't like this word, perspective.

Michael is enjoying the sun.

MICHAEL:

This sun makes me feel very much alive. You know, in many ways, we're all very much alike.

RUSTY:

I hate to disappoint you there, Michael, but look at the three of us. We ain't nothing alike. What we got in common you could stuff in my underwear.

KEESIC:

That small, huh?

MICHAEL:

We're all Indian.

KEESIC:

I am Odawa, not this "Indian."

MICHAEL:

Okay then, we're all Odawa.

KEESIC:

> No.

MICHAEL:

> Pardon?

KEESIC:

> No. I don't think you are Odawa. Or you, either.
> Everything I have heard today is not Odawa.

RUSTY:

> Hey, I was born on the reserve. I am so Odawa and
> Ojibway. I got a card and everything.

KEESIC:

> It's more than blood. I am very saddened by what
> has happened to my people.

MICHAEL:

> We've survived and we're getting stronger.

KEESIC:

> Then why are we speaking this English? Do we not
> have our old tongue? The Odawa tongue? Why are
> we speaking this English? Is this the language of
> these white people?

MICHAEL:

> That's not fair. I wanted to learn the language, but
> nobody speaks it anymore.

KEESIC:

> *To Rusty.* Do you speak your language?

RUSTY:

> I can count up to 10. Next year though, I'm taking
> the language in school. There's a new course.

KEESIC:

A course? In school? What does that mean?

RUSTY:

I guess it means I'll be spending an hour a day in school learning to speak Indian.

KEESIC:

You take time out to learn it? Why is it not spoken freely in your villages?

RUSTY:

I don't know. I guess there's not a need for it any more. English is spoken everywhere and we were sort of dragged along with it.

KEESIC:

But our language is formed by our thoughts. Our thinking forms our words. I do not like this language, English. There is no beauty in it. In our language, when you talk about the earth or the forest, you can smell the leaves around you, feel the grass beneath your feet. Until our language is spoken again and rituals and ceremonies followed, then there are no more Odawa.

MICHAEL:

That's not fair. I know I'm Indian. Just because I don't like muskrat or moose meat is no reason to say I'm not Indian.

KEESIC:

Odawa.

MICHAEL:

Odawa then.

*Michael pushes Keesic's shoulder in frustration.
Retaliating, Keesic pushes Michael and a fight
ensues. Rusty gets in there and is attacked by
both boys. He extricates himself quickly.*

RUSTY:

Okay, okay, fine.

MICHAEL:

Every culture must progress. You'd be amazed and
pleased to see what we've achieved. Odawa are no
longer starving in the bush, or dying of some
disease. We are in control of our own destiny.

KEESIC:

But weren't we always?

MICHAEL:

Not until we achieved self-government in the
2020s.

KEESIC:

Self-government? When did we lose it?

MICHAEL:

In the late 1700s and early 1800s I believe.

KEESIC:

What happened to us?

MICHAEL:

We signed treaties with the white government and
were put on reserves of land and left there to die.

KEESIC:

But not any more?

MICHAEL:

No. We control our own paths again.

KEESIC:

At what cost? We lost ourselves to regain something we shouldn't have lost in the first place. There are no more Odawa.

MICHAEL:

How can you say that? It's not true.

KEESIC:

An Odawa would never let nobody take the land.

MICHAEL:

They did.

KEESIC:

They did not.

RUSTY:

They did, Keesic.

KEESIC:

They did not. I don't believe you. What would they have to gain by selling the land? Something nobody can own?

MICHAEL:

Some of these white people got them drunk and made them sign something called treaties.

KEESIC:

Drunk? With this thing called beer?

MICHAEL:

Something like that. Others signed to save their people, to keep what little land they could to live on.

KEESIC:

Didn't they fight?

MICHAEL:

They did, but there were too many of them.

KEESIC:

I can't believe they are more powerful than the Odawa.

MICHAEL:

In some ways they were. But you're wrong, Keesic. No matter what you may think of us, we still exist. Changed, but Odawa.

KEESIC:

You may have Odawa blood in your veins but do you have the heart to pump it?

MICHAEL:

We're better Odawa than you ever were.

KEESIC:

I don't think so.

MICHAEL:

It was an Odawa doctor who discovered the cure for the common cold.

KEESIC:

We never had the common cold.

RUSTY:

> For two people who claim to know so much about us, you sure are stupid.

MICHAEL:

> If anybody here were to be classified as stupid, I'm sure it would be you.

> *Rusty looks at Michael, then at Keesic, then at the vista of his home.*

RUSTY:

> Where are we standing?

MICHAEL:

> Pardon?

RUSTY:

> Where are we standing?

> *Keesic and Michael look at each other, confused.*

RUSTY:

> We're on Dreamer's Rock. And what is Dreamer's Rock a part of? *More confused looks.* It's part of the land, part of Mother Earth. My Uncle Stan once told me that it all comes back to that. The Odawa, and I guess other Indians, are the land, of the land. The land is the basis for everything. We have survived not just on the land, but with it.

KEESIC:

> How can you know the meaning of survival, you who have never known hunger?

RUSTY:

I survive in my time, you survive in yours. You do it by hunting in the bush, I do it by working in a snack bar, and he probably does it through space-age stuff. The tools may change but the idea stays the same. The point is, we've survived. We're still here today.

MICHAEL:

And tomorrow.

Rusty pauses as he collects his thoughts.

RUSTY:

Yesterday I wouldn't have thought all this was possible. Yesterday it would have been another day of the Flintstones, working at the snack bar, and maybe a beer afterwards.

MICHAEL:

And now?

RUSTY:

All I know is I came up here to get drunk and be alone for a while. So much for that idea. I never thought about all this Indian stuff before. I just sort of took it for granted. I guess I have some more thinking to do. I think the main thing about being Indian or Odawa is ... we're better-looking.

All the boys smile.

KEESIC:

That will always be true.

RUSTY:

Some things will never change.

MICHAEL:

Rusty.

RUSTY:

Yo Dude, what can I do you for?

MICHAEL:

I have something I want to give you. Actually, I'm returning it to you, even before you gave it to me.

Michael gives him a small, rusted container.

RUSTY:

What is it?

He opens it, takes out an old newspaper clipping and reads.

RUSTY:

This says I'm going to be the first Grand Chief of the Aboriginal Government. And it's dated 2023. I'll be 50 years old. *It sinks in.* Holy. I'll be old. Damn. Guess this means I have to go back to school. And I thought I'd be free next year.

KEESIC:

All things come with a price, Rusty.

RUSTY:

Awed. Wow. Me, Grand Chief.

KEESIC:

> That's a pretty powerful title, Rusty. I hope you
> can find it in yourself to live up to it.

RUSTY:

> I can't even drive a car yet and already I'm running
> a government.

> *Keesic takes something from around his neck. It is
> a hide pouch.*

KEESIC:

> I, too, am not without a gift. I want you to wear it
> around your neck.

RUSTY:

> What is it?

KEESIC:

> Weekah root. It will keep you strong and healthy.

> *Keesic places it around Rusty's neck. Rusty fingers
> the pouch.*

RUSTY:

> Thanks guys. Thanks a lot, but I don't have any-
> thing to give you.

MICHAEL:

> Don't worry, your time to give will come.

> *The sound of the crow cawing can be heard again.*

KEESIC:

Rusty, this is your summer. And spring belongs before it, and fall afterwards. Every season has its time and I think it's time to return to those places. I think Toronto has come to an end.

Rusty holds his hand out in an effort to shake Keesic's hand.

RUSTY:

It's been interesting, Keesic. That's all I can say.

Keesic looks puzzled at Rusty's outstretched hand.

MICHAEL:

You're supposed to shake hands.

Keesic looks at his own hand and shakes it vigorously like he's trying to get something off it. Rusty and Michael laugh as Rusty grabs Keesic's hand. Suddenly, when they touch, they are all thrown to the ground. Keesic starts to cough again. Rusty slaps him on the back.

RUSTY:

You okay? Hey man, you all right?

KEESIC:

Stat-ta-ha. Ngashtoon chi nishnaabemyaan miin-waa. [I can speak my language again.]

RUSTY:

I thought you said you couldn't speak it any more.

Keesic speaks to them in Indian, telling them they must pray. He places the boys carefully, facing the east, and begins a final prayer of thanksgiving to the Creator for allowing them to meet across time on this sacred spot.

At the end of the prayer, Rusty sinks to the rock, holds his weekah pouch with one hand and drums a beat on the rock with the other. He sings a song in Indian about hearing the voice of the people, so far away. During the song, Michael and Keesic leave the rock and disappear within it. At the end of the song, Rusty opens his eyes. He is alone. He goes to pick up his knapsack and beneath it he finds a crow feather. He holds the feather up to the sky, turning four times, saluting the Four Directions. Then he moves off. Just before leaving, he places his hand respectfully on the rock.

RUSTY:

Ah, meeg-wetch. [Thank you.]

THE END

Education is
Our Right

Production Notes

Education is Our Right had its first performance in East Main, Quebec, on 4 February 1990; it was produced by De-Ba-Jeh-Mu-Jig Theatre Group, Wikwemikong Unceded Reserve, Manitoulin Island, under the direction of Larry Lewis. The following cast appeared in multiple roles:

Deborah Anwhatin
Bruce Armstrong
Jack Burning
Mark Seabrook

Education is Our Right is a play about the times it was written in. The play was conceived, written, and produced less than a year after Pierre Cadieux, then the Federal Minister of Indian and Northern Affairs, announced a cap on post-secondary education for Native students. Needless to say, this announcement did not go over well in Native communities, and there is still much discussion over this controversial policy.

All of the vignettes in this play are based on real incidents (with the exception of the future segments that hopefully will never come to pass). There was a walk to the nation's capital, a hunger strike in Ottawa, residential schools, and Elders who told wonderful and educational stories. There is very little fiction in this drama.

At the time of publication, little has changed in the government's policy. There is, however, hope for the future.

Education Is Our Right is an easy play to produce but a difficult play to act. Since it was created for the purpose of touring not just by car but by plane, the set and costumes had to be light and easy to transport. As a result, the set is minimal. In the original production, a handful of numbered and lettered building blocks of various sizes were the main components of the set. These could be rearranged in any number of configurations depending on the scene.

Since many of the numerous characters in the play are on stage for only a few moments, it its suggested that each actor carry a variety of roles. Costumes should be used and exploited to help differentiate among the various supporting characters.

Cast of Characters
(in order of appearance)

Ebenezer Cadieux,	39
Minister of Indian Affairs	
Young woman	22
Spirit of Knowledge	Ageless
Education Past	35
Elder	60
Young girl	13
Teacher	40
Sagateh	8
Education Present	26
Father	37
Boy	16
Reporter	30
Eric	21
Want & Ignorance	Ageless
Education Future	45
Man	35
Woman	25
Street Indian	48
Reserve Indian	29
Integrator	33

Location:
Otter Lake, a fictional central Ontario Native reserve; a variety of other places.

Time:
A cold winter day in January 1990; other time periods.

*A very professional and governmental looking
man makes his way through the crowd to the
center. He is carrying a briefcase and gives a
professional smile to everyone he passes. Occasionally he stops to shake hands, as if he is cam-
paigning.*

*Eventually he makes his way up to a speaker's
podium. He straightens his tie, an action that
becomes a nervous habit throughout the performance. This is MR. EBENEZER CADIEUX, Minister
of Indian Affairs.*

*He smiles warmly at the people, opens his brief-
case, takes out some notes, and begins his ad-
dress.*

CADIEUX:
My name is Ebenezer Cadieux, the Minister of
Indian Affairs. One of the fringe benefits of my
position is that it allows me to meet interesting
and real people like yourselves. I've never been to
Otter Lake before, but getting here was utter
confusion. *He laughs at his own joke and nerv-
ously adjusts his tie.* No doubt many of you have
heard over the past few months about my plan to
put a cap on post-secondary schooling. I thought
this would be a good time to shed some well-
deserved light on the subject and dispel some of
the rumors surrounding this plan, and I have
chosen your beautiful community, Otter Lake, to
begin. Now, my decision was based on some
serious thinking.

*A young woman stands up in the audience, pad
and pen in hand.*

YOUNG WOMAN:
> Mr. Cadieux, did you bother to find out how our Native people felt about this decision?

CADIEUX:
> We consulted most of the Aboriginal organizations and local band governments with an early draft of the proposal.

YOUNG WOMAN:
> And what was the result?

CADIEUX:
> I believe the first reaction was *He mumbles.* less than favorable.

YOUNG WOMAN:
> Say what?

CADIEUX:
> *Annoyed.* I said, their first reaction was *A little louder.* less than favorable.

YOUNG WOMAN:
> They didn't like it, but you just went ahead anyway? Just like you government people always do.

CADIEUX:
> We at the department felt that the Native people held a particularly prejudicial point of view, that of maintaining the status quo, rather than seeing the need for change. Therefore, their comments had to be taken with a grain of salt.

The young woman stops writing, not sure if she can believe her ears. Cadieux is getting noticeably more nervous, and keeps fiddling with his tie.

YOUNG WOMAN:

Prejudicial point of view? Grain of salt? Excuse me, Mr. Minister, but we have every right to want the status quo maintained.

CADIEUX:

You do not have that right!

YOUNG WOMAN:

Oh yeah? Think again, Mr. Minister.

She moves up the aisle with force. Cadieux jumps out of her path, and runs about as she pursues him quietly, and with dignity. Finally he is cornered.

CADIEUX:

Terrified. Who are you?

YOUNG WOMAN:

A second-year political science student. What about treaty rights?

CADIEUX:

It's true that education is guaranteed in most treaties, but you have to understand that when these treaties were signed, things were different. Education then meant on-reserve education, not post-secondary.

YOUNG WOMAN:
> I don't remember reading that in any of the treaties.

CADIEUX:
> Times change. So do people. And so do interpretations. The treaties are open to interpretation.

YOUNG WOMAN:
> Answer me this, Mr. Minister. If only certain Native people are eligible for this money, what happens to all the other Native students?

CADIEUX:
> Are there no scholarships, no bursaries? They have the same chance that every non-Native student has.

YOUNG WOMAN:
> Scholarships, bursaries. You just don't understand, so you?

> *Frustrated, she turns and makes her way down the aisle.*

CADIEUX:
> Young lady, just a minute ...

YOUNG WOMAN:
> Creep. *To herself.* It's such a shame when cousins marry.

> *Cadieux is terribly offended. He begins to pack up.*

CADIEUX:
> I'm sorry, but you really must excuse me.

Cadieux closes his briefcase and is about to leave when a big booming voice comes from behind the audience. It is the Spirit of Knowledge. He is tall, with an ethereal quality. He floats rather than walks.

SPIRIT OF KNOWLEDGE:
Why?!

Cadieux looks momentarily perplexed by the sudden appearance of the Spirit.

CADIEUX:
Because I have another engagement elsewhere.

Cadieux starts to move but finds his feet stuck to the ground. He tries to move them, only to discover that his hands are attached to his briefcase and he can't let go.

SPIRIT OF KNOWLEDGE:
Why?

CADIEUX:
Uh, excuse me. Could someone give me a hand? I seem to be having a problem.

Cadieux fumbles around for a moment as the Spirit walks closer. He gets his first good look at the Spirit.

CADIEUX:
My, you sure are a big one. Could ... could you give me a hand?

SPIRIT OF KNOWLEDGE:

A hand, and much more. A hand is only the beginning. Picture a hand reaching out for direction, a path. A whole universe can be created by a hand picking up a book, or learning a new craft. Yes, a hand can be the beginning.

CADIEUX:

Who are you?

The Spirit starts moving around Cadieux in a slow, hypnotizing way.

SPIRIT OF KNOWLEDGE:

I am the keeper of all knowledge. And in that knowledge, salvation can be found. Salvation not only of the soul, but of the mind and spirit. I have a question for you, Mr. Cadieux, a very important one. Why are you limiting the chance for knowledge?

CADIEUX:

Almost miserable. Oh no, not another one. Look, we in Ottawa didn't wake up one morning and say to ourselves, "Hey, let's be mean to the Indians today!"

Cadieux opens his briefcase with a flourish and pulls out some papers.

CADIEUX:

Here, read it for yourself. It's all there.

The Spirit takes the paper and throws it up in the air.

SPIRIT OF KNOWLEDGE:

That speech doesn't interest me. It looks only at the surface, not the base underneath it. Money is not the issue, Mr. Cadieux, the people are. You see the effects of only one part of the process, not the cause of it all. I think it is time for you to visit the cause. And if you ask why, because.

Closing his briefcase, Cadieux steps back.

CADIEUX:

I've got appointments. I am the Minister of Indian Affairs, you know.

SPIRIT OF KNOWLEDGE:

No, you are just a student. And today you will be visited by three teachers. These teachers will take you along the trail of knowledge so that you will understand why things are the way they are.

CADIEUX:

Who are these teachers? Why should I go with them?

SPIRIT OF KNOWLEDGE:

They are the Spirits of Education Past, Present, and Future. They, above all, will help you.

CADIEUX:

Getting indignant. I don't need help, I'm in the government. And if anybody does need help around here, Mr. Spirit of Knowledge, go take a look at yourself.

The Spirit starts backing up, going out of sight.

SPIRIT OF KNOWLEDGE:

> *Holding up three fingers.* Three Spirits. Remember, Mr. Cadieux, three Spirits.

> *The Spirit disappears, leaving Cadieux confused. He follows a few steps, looking around a bit, then shrugs. He kneels down, opens his briefcase, and starts to pick up some of the scattered papers.*

CADIEUX:

> I'm a politician. I don't need to learn anything. Imagine. *Imitating the Spirit of Knowledge.* "I am the keeper of all knowledge." Who does he think he is, Pierre Trudeau? *He looks at his watch.* Oh my goodness, I'm going to be late. So much for the Twilight Zone Secondary School. *He grabs the last few papers.* If I hurry, I can just about make it.

> *He closes his briefcase and stands up ready to leave. As he turns to exit he finds his way blocked by a tall, traditionally dressed (by Hollywood clichéd standards) Indian who stands there, arms folded, trying to look regal, like a cigar-store Indian.*

CADIEUX:

> Holy Mulroney! It's an Indian.

> *They stare at each other for a moment. Cadieux is unsure of himself.*

CADIEUX:

> Where did you come from? *No answer.* Hello? Excuse me, who are you? *No answer.* Yoo-hoo. Anybody in there? Do you speak English? Parlez-vous francais?

*Education Past comes to life. He brings his arms
down and nods at Cadieux. From this point on he
talks like Tonto, monosyllabically, using grunts
and nods to convey answers.*

PAST:

Me speak good English. How about you?

CADIEUX:

I speak it good   *Corrects himself.*   uh, fine. Who
are you? What are you doing here?

PAST:

Me Spirit of Education Past. Here to show you
things. Important things. Things you should know.

CADIEUX:

You're crazy.

PAST:

Shrugs.   Maybe. But we all crazy one way or
another. That half the fun of it.

CADIEUX:

What are you talking about? I'm not crazy.

PAST:

You work for government. That crazy.

CADIEUX:

Hey.   *Feels his suit.*   This is a $700 suit. Now that
ain't crazy.

PAST:

Points.   That tie is. But not matter, we not here
for wardrobe reason. You need direction.

CADIEUX:

I do, huh?

Education Past begins setting up a scene with hides and an open fire.

PAST:

In order find forward direction, it help look behind first.

Cadieux shakes his head for a moment.

CADIEUX:

Why do you talk like that?

PAST:

Like what?

CADIEUX:

Like that. It's irritating. Talk right.

Education Past points to a television that has materialized.

PAST:

You know that box?

Cadieux looks at it closely.

CADIEUX:

It's a television. An old one, too. Haven't seen one of those in years, not since I was a kid.

PAST:

Hmmmm, you not as stupid as people say.

CADIEUX:

> *Smiles.*   Thank you.   *It dawns on him.*   Hey,
> wait a moment!

PAST:

> This your television when boy. You spend many
> hours looking here. Saw many things, made you
> laugh, cry, scare you.

CADIEUX:

> Oh wow, I remember, that was so long ago.

PAST:

> Many winters ago.

CADIEUX:

> I used to love this thing. I'd watch everything.

PAST:

> Including cowboys and Indians.

CADIEUX:

> The Lone Ranger and Tonto, Bonanza, Gunsmoke!
> And all those old movies. I remember them.

PAST:

> And what you remember about them? About the
> Indians?
>
> *It dawns on Cadieux and he turns quickly to
> Education Past.*

CADIEUX:

> They all talked like you.

*Education Past nods, content, the point of his
lesson received.*

PAST:

Huhh, good, you remember.

CADIEUX:

That still doesn't explain why you are talking like
this. That was a long time ago.

PAST:

But you grew up thinking we talk like this. Your
subconscious continue to think this about us. Part
of you still think we simple people, barely grasp
language. So me come to you as you grew up, as
Tonto or thousand other television Indians. And
like this, me take you on journey.

CADIEUX:

I don't want to go.

PAST:

Tough. Life a bummer. Take my hand.

*Cadieux looks at Education Past's outstretched
hand, then back at his face.*

CADIEUX:

Why?

By this time Education Past is getting frustrated.

PAST:

Because if I bring foot up it cramp. Just take hand,
okay?

Cadieux reaches out and grabs Education Past's hand.

CADIEUX:

What now?

PAST:

All things have beginning, middle, and end. We go to beginning, back when Elders taught and children learned. Knowledge family and community responsibility.

CADIEUX:

Okay, Spirit of Education Past, how come you can say "community responsibility" but not get your personal pronouns right?

PAST:

Shrugs.   Me not make rules. That not important. Look!

Education Past points over to the side where there is a small campfire. An old man and a young girl are sitting around it. It's a cold winter night and the two are huddled up in blankets or skins. The young girl, sitting enraptured by the old man, occasionally pokes the fire.

CADIEUX:

Who that?   *Corrects himself.*   Who's that?

PAST:

Does it matter?

CADIEUX:

What year is this?

PAST:

Does it matter?

CADIEUX:

What does matter then?

PAST:

Smiles.   Hmmm. Listen, and you learn.

The Elder is in the midst of telling a legend to the young girl.

ELDER:

And then one day this crazy old Nanabush was walking through the forest. He had trouble in his heart and mischief in his eyes. And in that forest he heard a noise, a small little noise, a peeping of a noise, and he stopped. He looked around but didn't see anything. But there was the mysterious peeping again, and it came from the sky. So Nanabush looked up and way up, I mean way up, was this bird's nest. Being naturally curious, Nanabush climbed to the top of that big tree, and do you know what he found?   *The little girl shakes her head.*   A nest full of little baby birds crying out for their mother. Now that Nanabush, with that mischief in his eyes, did something very silly. He thought to himself, "What do you do with a nest full of birds?" So he came to a conclusion.   *The little girl nods eagerly.*   He shit on them. Yep, that crazy old Nanabush took a shit on those poor defenseless birds and had a good laugh over it. In fact he laughed about it for a long time. Well, it wasn't over then. Later that summer Nanabush was out walking in that very same forest when he came to a stream. It wasn't a very big stream but it was wide enough to be annoying. So Nanabush decided to jump the stream. But to do that he had to clear a path and he spent all day preparing for that big jump. Near the end of that day he was ready. It took four tries before he knew he would make it, but as he was sailing over the stream he heard a voice call out his name. Nanabush looked up and boom, he lost his balance and went splash into the stream. He was a very wet and sorry-looking Nanabush. And those voices? Nanabush looked up and saw it was those very same birds that he had shit on not so long ago, but all were grown up and flying. They had the last laugh.

Cadieux turns to Education Past, upset. The Elder and the young girl disappear.

CADIEUX:
> You brought me here for this? A children's story?

PAST:
> You understand story?

CADIEUX:
> It's hard not to. It is a very simple story.

PAST:
> Sometimes, best lessons in life simple.

CADIEUX:
> All right then, I won't go shitting on any birds any more. Can we go now?

Education Past shakes his head.

PAST:

No, you still not understand. This how my people learn in beginning. They learn from family, not strangers. Everything they need here and around them. They self-sufficient.

CADIEUX:

I get the point. But things change. This kind of life isn't possible any more, just like your kind of Indian doesn't exist any more. Times change.

PAST:

Yes, time change, but not always for better. You people come to our shores, everything change. Nothing same any more, including education.

Cadieux is smug. He starts pacing confidently.

CADIEUX:

See, I told you. You are no longer freezing or starving in the woods. All your problems were solved by us. And what the cap on funding will do is force you to rely on your own initiative. I think we've spoon-fed you too long as it is, really I do.

PAST:

Me sure you do. Spoon-fed. All problems solved, eh? I don't think so. Amazing how quickly people forget.

CADIEUX:

Forget what?

PAST:

Not so long ago. You first tried educate us, your way. You tried make us white.

CADIEUX:

> I'm not sure I understand.

Education Past looks very solemn and paces a bit. He talks in a low whisper.

PAST:

> Residential schools.

Cadieux steps back, almost panicked.

CADIEUX:

> I had nothing to do with those, I wasn't even born when they started. I only learned about them a few years ago.

PAST:

> Yes, you to blame, maybe not personally. But people in power like you decide what good for Indians, though not caring what Indians think.

Both are silent for a moment; Cadieux thinks.

CADIEUX:

> These residential schools, were they as bad as everyone says?

PAST:

> Children kidnapped, taken to religious schools. Beaten, sexually abused, all approved and encouraged by government. This is a way of education?

CADIEUX:

> People make mistakes.

PAST:

Entire generations of culture, spirit dead, because of government decision about our education. Sound familiar, Mr. Cadieux?

Education Past shakes his head remorsefully. He points to a classroom in a residential school. There is a white male teacher and an Indian girl student in the classroom. The girl looks terrified and keeps her eyes down. Meanwhile the teacher looks very strict.

TEACHER:

What is your name?   *No response.*   I'm waiting. Do you speak English, girl? Well, do you?

The girl nods slightly.

TEACHER:

That's a change. Then speak it.   *No response. Louder.*   Speak it. What is your name?

The girl responds, her voice small and cracking, her eyes still down.

GIRL:

Sagateh.

TEACHER:

Your English name.

The girl falters, not knowing how to respond.

SAGATEH:

Sagateh?

The teacher looks at her closely for a moment.

TEACHER:
I see, no Christian name. *Thinks.*   Agnes, you can be Agnes. Do you hear me, Agnes?

SAGATEH:
Sagateh.

The teacher grabs her by the shoulders and shakes her harshly. The little girl reacts in fear.

TEACHER:
Now you listen to me, you little heathen. In this school you will speak English and only English, none of that gobbledygook you call a language. Do you understand me?

For the first time the girl looks up, half in fear and half in confusion.

SAGATEH:
Yes.

TEACHER:
I didn't hear you. Louder.

SAGATEH:
A little louder.   Yes.

The teacher, satisfied, turns and walks to his seat. The little girl sticks her tongue out at him when he turns his back.

TEACHER:

Very good, Agnes. That's a beginning. Now since you will be staying at our school, quite probably till you turn 16, there are a few rules you must know. When a member of the staff talks to you, you will do what you are told when you are told to. Is that understood?

The girl nods.

TEACHER:

You will be given a bed and a set of clothes. These are to be kept clean at all times, as well as yourself. Classes will be in the morning and chores will be assigned for the afternoon. You will be expected to attend church services on a regular basis.

SAGATEH:

My brother ...

The teacher checks some papers on his desk, adjusts his glasses.

TEACHER:

Oh yes, you were sent here with a brother. You may see him on Sundays. Under no circumstances are you to speak anything other than English, or practice any rituals that are not of a Christian origin. Any infractions will result in physical punishment. Understand?

The girl, looking even more confused, duly nods.

TEACHER:

Good. Here at the school, we believe that in order to save the person, we must first destroy the Indian. In the years to come, you will grow to appreciate our efforts.

The student gets up and walks toward the door. The teacher passes by her. As the girl closes the door, she sticks out her tongue again as a form of rebellion. During the following dialogue, the girl remains staring off after the teacher.

PAST:

Hmmm. Me no think me like progress.

Cadieux is at a loss for words.

CADIEUX:

I didn't know it was like this, but I'm sure the intention was good.

PAST:

What they say about road to Hell?

CADIEUX:

But that was years ago. Things have changed. You people have a say in your own education now.

PAST:

Like in your cap on funding. Some say!

Cadieux is silent for a moment. He stares off to where the little girl was sitting.

CADIEUX:

Whatever happened to that little girl?

PAST:

What it matter? Just a number in DIA book.

CADIEUX:

More insistent.   What happened to her?!

PAST:

She live on reserve now, old woman with lots of grandchildren.

Cadieux breathes a sigh of relief. He had expected worse. He turns to Education Past, almost confidently.

CADIEUX:

There, see, it didn't turn out so bad.

PAST:

Course, she still limp a lot.

CADIEUX:

Pardon?

PAST:

Six months after arrive at school. She run away, in winter. Frostbite find her before they do. They took off half of foot.

Cadieux is visibly taken aback.

CADIEUX:

That beautiful little girl?   *Education Past nods.* But why did she run away, and in winter? That's stupid.

PAST:

What you do in same circumstances? I think you try run too. Her body broke, but not spirit.

CADIEUX:

I didn't know ...

Education Past shakes his head slowly, knowingly.

PAST:

Of course not, you just responsible for Indians, not have to like or know.

CADIEUX:

That's a nasty comment. I didn't know Spirits could be nasty.

PAST:

You try talking like this for all history, you get plenty nasty.

CADIEUX:

So am I supposed to learn anything from this? Am I supposed to wake up in the morning with a ray of sunshine and see the world in a whole new light? Am I supposed to have a whole change of philosophy, join the NDP or something?

PAST:

No, that too radical.

CADIEUX:

What? Joining the NDP?

PAST:

> All of it. You a person, and as person, you have decision to make. Some decisions matter of mind, others matter of heart. Two not necessarily go hand in hand.

CADIEUX:

> Welcome to the government.

PAST:

> No thank you. It time for me leave now. Me show you all I could and should. The past behind you, and so am I.
>
> *Education Past starts to back away.*

CADIEUX:

> What happens now? What happens to me?
>
> *Education Past shakes his head and smiles as he disappears.*

PAST:

> Not my department.
>
> *Cadieux is left on stage by himself, feeling alone.*

CADIEUX:

> I wish I was back in Ottawa. Nothing ever happens there.   *He looks around again.*   So what now? I guess I'm supposed to wait for another Spirit or something.
>
> *So Cadieux waits for a long awkward moment. He starts biting his nails. After a moment, he starts to get frustrated and begins pacing.*

CADIEUX:

Ghost! Spirit! Whatever you are! Can we, like, move on here? *To himself.* I hate a Spirit without a watch.

PRESENT:

Yeah, what d'ya want?

Cadieux wheels around and finds himself facing a pretty young girl, the Spirit of Education Present, dressed in a contemporary powwow dancing outfit including a shawl. She has an angry, impatient attitude about her and gives a lot of lip.

CADIEUX:

My God!

PRESENT:

Nah, she's busy. *She laughs at her own joke.* So what d'ya want already? I ain't got all day.

CADIEUX:

You're the Spirit of ...

PRESENT:

Education Present, Einstein. Get to the point. I'm supposed to be at a powwow already, you want something or what?

Cadieux is taken aback by the Spirit's rather abrasive attitude. She is not a very likable Spirit and he's not sure how to answer her question.

CADIEUX::

I'm not sure. I wasn't exactly told what to expect from you.

PRESENT:

Wait a minute. You're that Cadieux fellow, ain't ya? *Cadieux nods.* That's today? Ah nuts. I've really got to get an appointment book. *She looks at her watch.* Ah hell, there goes the grand entry, right out the window. *She looks at him with anger.* Thanks Cadieux.

CADIEUX:

I'm sorry ... I think.

PRESENT:

Yeah, yeah, save it for your mother. Damn, I was looking forward to that powwow too.

CADIEUX:

Spirits go to powwows?

PRESENT:

Imitating him. Yes, Spirits go to powwows. *To the sky.* Where do they find these people?

CADIEUX:

I was at a powwow once. I don't remember seeing you there.

PRESENT:

But you weren't looking for me, were you? Besides, don't we all look alike to you? I've always had this theory about the inability of blue eyes to accurately see brown skin. Let one of your anthropologists check that out. *She looks at him.* So you're Ebenezer Cadieux.

The Spirit stands there for a moment assessing Cadieux, her eyes covering every inch of him, boring into his mind. Cadieux begins to feel self-conscious.

CADIEUX:
Is there something wrong?

PRESENT:
I don't think you want a serious answer to that. After all the trouble you've caused, you're not very popular at the office.

CADIEUX:
You've got an office?

PRESENT:
Yeah, we start work at 9 and work till infinite. Education Past is right down the hall from me. Boy, he really doesn't like you, you know. He told me the other day, "Me like drop kick skinny white man." *She laughs lightly.* All right, to business. I suppose I got to show you around a bit.

CADIEUX:
No you don't. I'd be more than happy to go home.

PRESENT:
I bet you would, but that's not how things work around here. You cost me a good powwow, Cadieux, so I'm gonna put you through the works.

CADIEUX:
I suppose you want to take a chunk out of me too.

PRESENT:
Smiles enigmatically. I'm a lady.

Cadieux looks around apprehensively; he knows what's coming.

CADIEUX:
I take it I'm to take your arm.

PRESENT:
You kidding? I never let a man touch me on our first astral projection. Just grab the shawl.

Cadieux touches the shawl and they find themselves in the kitchen of a house. A young Native boy is arguing with his father.

FATHER:
You'll lose a whole year. You'll have to repeat it.

BOY:
No I won't. And even if I do, it's worth it.

FATHER:
I don't like fooling around with your school year. These days you need every advantage you can get. If you go on this march to Ottawa ...

BOY:
It's not a march, it's a walk.

FATHER:
Whatever. If you go, you'll lose another three weeks of school. My answer is no. I'm sorry. There's too much at stake.

BOY:

> If something isn't done, there may be no school after I graduate. We'll all be scrambling and fighting to go to university.

FATHER:

> My responsibility is to you. Everybody else can look after themselves.

BOY:

> Ever since I can remember, that's how it's been around here. It's like fingers on a hand, all squabbling. Dad, for the first time in a hell of a long time, everybody here wants to do something together. The fingers are coming together. Half of the reserve is marching to Ottawa. I have to be a part of it.

FATHER:

> *Sighs.* Why do you do these things? Why can't you just run around and chase girls like other boys?

BOY:

> Well, on this march, the girls will only be walking, it'll be easier to catch them.

> *The boy tries a hesitant smile to relieve the tension. The father reciprocates with a small smile.*

FATHER:

> What am I gonna do with you?

BOY:

> Let me go?

FATHER:

> What do you think your mother will say? She's a
> hard woman to convince about things like this.
> She still thinks rock and roll is a fad. The fact that
> she voted PC will make it worse.

BOY:

> Will you help me convince her?

FATHER:

> You think you're going to make a difference? You
> think anybody is going to listen to you?

BOY:

> How am I going to know who is listening if I never
> speak? You always told me I should stand up for
> what I think is right. I think this is right. I want to
> walk. I want to walk beside you.

FATHER:

> Me! And take time off work and lose my job and
> who is going to feed the family? It's old dreams,
> boy. You won't make a difference.

BOY:

> You're getting too comfortable in your old age.
> Where's that warrior spirit?

The father thinks for a moment.

FATHER:

> That's pretty far away, Ottawa.

Cadieux turns and looks at the Spirit.

CADIEUX:

I've heard of this march.

PRESENT:

Hundreds of people, walking from Manitoulin Island to Ottawa, a trip of several hundred miles, I believe.

CADIEUX:

People just don't understand. Sometimes harsh and drastic decisions have to be made. The education budget kept doubling and tripling every few years. The money had to stop at some point.

PRESENT:

Yeah right. Like defense budgets and foreign aid. Your government spends a fortune in foreign aid, but cuts back on the aid to its own original inhabitants. Shame, shame, Mr. Conservative. Would you rather help finance the destruction of the Amazon rainforests, or perhaps create a new Cree doctor, or an Ojibway writer, or a Mohawk architect? I think priorities are the issue here, Mr. Cadieux.

CADIEUX:

The treaties state, and I quote ...

PRESENT:

Excuse me but I don't need to hear a white government official quoting treaties to defend a position. You guys don't exactly have a great track record concerning treaties. It's kinda like Colonel Sanders selling life insurance to chickens.

CADIEUX:

Spluttering.   But, but, but ...

PRESENT:

So much for the term "smooth as a politician."
Take a look, Cadieux, at the ground swell of people
reacting to your decision. And look who's here.
The boy's argument was quite impressive. He'd
make a wonderful politician if he could make it to
school.

*Cadieux gives the Spirit a nasty look. The boy is
now walking. He looks tired, but determined.*

BOY:

Wow! Two hundred miles in the same pair of
sneakers. My feet must stink.   *He turns to a
fellow walker.*   What do you mean, that's why
you're changing tents? At least I don't need a
chisel to take off my socks.

The boy's father approaches.

FATHER:

Son.

BOY:

Dad! What are you doing here? Is Mom with you?

FATHER:

Yeah. She's back there talking with your Auntie
Ethel trying to get that 20 bucks she borrowed. We
may never see her again.

BOY:

But what are you doing here?

FATHER:

> We've been watching you guys on the news and in the papers. And I guess we began to get guilty feelings. We tried to fight them off as long as we could, but here we are.

BOY:

> I can't believe Mom's gonna walk. She'd take a taxi to the bathroom if she could. I'm impressed. You're gonna do this for me?

FATHER:

> Not only for you. Your little sister will be going to high school in a few years. You started me thinking about her future. I didn't like some of the things that popped into my head. She may not have the chance to do something like this, it might be over and done with. But I want her to know we tried. *He smiles.* And I thought the sixties were over. So, how are things going?

BOY:

> We got about another 10 days ahead of us.

FATHER:

> And where do people sleep when they stop walking?

BOY:

> You and Mom can share my tent.

FATHER:

> Tents?! Your mother? Well. It's been a few years, but sure. *He listens to someone off at the side*

and frowns. What does your buddy mean, "I'll be sorry?"

The Spirit is starting to take off her traditional outfit.

PRESENT:
That was only a little while ago. Did you see them?

CADIEUX:
I was ... unavailable at the time.

The Spirit points to her face.

PRESENT:
See this face? Notice there's not the vaguest impression of surprise on it?

CADIEUX:
I don't have the time to see everyone who comes to my office with a complaint. If I did that, I'd never get any work done. It's a matter of job efficiency.

PRESENT:
I thought you were supposed to be accountable and available to the public, since theoretically you're supposed to represent them.

CADIEUX:
That's what elections are for.

PRESENT:
That's what elections are for. Is it no wonder that 90% of Indians don't vote?

Cadieux finally notices the Spirit getting undressed. She pulls the dress over her head. Underneath she's wearing shorts, running shoes, and a t-shirt. She stretches and looks more comfortable. She drapes the shawl over the bundle of discarded clothing.

PRESENT:

Ah! That feels better.

CADIEUX:

You people are always blowing things out of proportion. Whether it's land claims, the legal system, and now education. White people don't always get what they want, either.

PRESENT:

I'm not here to argue economic or philosophical viewpoints. If you want I can put you through to our Spirit of Race Relations.

CADIEUX:

Uh, no thanks.

PRESENT:

That's probably a good idea. If there's two things he can't stand, it's white people and racism.

CADIEUX:

Confused. Uh, yeah ...

PRESENT:

Looking at her watch. Anyways, we're falling behind schedule. We got to speed things up, I've got a hectic schedule to keep. It's not all powwows for this Spirit, you know. I'm backed up as it is.

CADIEUX:

How busy can a Spirit be? What are they going to do, fire you?

PRESENT:

There was a period when I had a lot of free time. No powwows, very little useful education, no nothing, everything was lost or dying. I almost went stir crazy from nothing to do. Now I'm so busy, it's great. *She sneers at him.* Till you came along.

CADIEUX:

I am sick and tired of always being the bad guy. For the last time, it was necessary.

The Spirit almost spits out her words.

PRESENT:

God, how many times have I heard those words?

CADIEUX:

What is your problem, lady? Ever since I met you, you've been acting like you're this short of breaking out into rabies. Your first words were "Yeah, what d'ya want?" I've never done anything against you. Why are you always acting so angry?

PRESENT:

You really want to know? Fine, I'll tell you. Ever since the second world war which your people started and my people helped fight, I've been breaking my back and my ass to help my people regain everything we've lost over the centuries. For the last couple of decades I was making fantastic

progress. Kids in universities, doctors, lawyers,
political leaders. But I guess that goes out the
window now, doesn't it?

*Mr. Cadieux turns away, throwing up his hands in
frustration.*

CADIEUX:
What's the use?

PRESENT:
That's the $64,000 question. By the way, you
hungry?

CADIEUX:
Not really, big breakfast. *Smiles greedily.* Government per diem.

PRESENT:
I see. When was the last time you were really
hungry?

CADIEUX:
Uh, Monday I guess. I had meetings all day and
had to miss lunch.

The Spirit pretends to be grief-stricken.

PRESENT:
You poor soul. Mulroney the fascist, eh. Well, Mr.
Cadieux, let me show you some other people who
skipped a few lunches. These are a group of kids,
Mr. Minister, that weren't afraid to put their
health on the line. Let's put it this way, Cadieux,
these are the kids that made you famous.

*Cadieux and the Spirit find themselves in a hotel
room. There's a young Native man about to be
interviewed by a television reporter. They are
sitting on a bed. The young man looks tired and
weak. The reporter is looking at the cameraman.*

REPORTER:

Are we ready, John?   Pause.   Okay, let's go in five.

*During the next five seconds the reporter straight-
ens her outfit and adjusts the mike to her face.
She then speaks to the camera.*

REPORTER:

It's been said that in today's day and age it's hard
to find young people who are committed to an
ideal. Here in Ottawa, there's a group of Native
kids who are willing to put their lives on the line
for something most people take for granted. The
right to education. These young people are on a
hunger strike to protest the government's new
legislation that will restrict the amount of money
available to educate Native students. I have Eric,
one of the hunger strikers, here with me.

She turns to the young man.

REPORTER:

Eric, how long has it been so far?

ERIC:

Today is our 35th day.

REPORTER:

Any sign of an ending?

ERIC:

> Not so far. The government is still ignoring us. But one good thing anyways, we've received a lot of support from the people, both Native and white.

REPORTER:

> And some criticisms too I understand. What do you have to say about the rumors that food has been smuggled to you here in this hotel room?

ERIC:

> In the last 35 days, I've lost about 25 pounds, and everybody else in this room has lost about the same. If you want, I can get you a "before" picture and you can compare. It hurts me, us, that people think that way. People are free to come and look under our beds for pizza cartons, all they'll find is dirty underwear. We aren't enjoying doing this, it hurts. Do all those people who think this is just a game know what it's like to wake up morning after morning with a gnawing pain in their stomach? Every time we look out that window we see restaurants as far as the eye can see, hot dog vendors, variety stores. You never realize how many food commercials there are on television until you're on a hunger strike. We can't watch it any more. Every day we think is our last day, that we can't hold on another day. But we do. The importance of what we're doing gives us that strength, that's all we got to hold on to.

REPORTER:

> The government's history of cost and budget slashing is well known. What makes this budget restriction different from the others?

ERIC:

Other than the fact the promise and guarantee of education is stated quite clearly in God knows how many treaties, the reason is simple. Educated Indians cause trouble. We know how to fight your way now. The government wants to stop that, stop the criticizing of its DIA policies and the fight over self-government. It wants to go back to the good old days when we did what we were told.

REPORTER:

And how does Ebenezer Cadieux, Minister of Indian Affairs, respond to your hunger strike?

ERIC:

How do you think? He refuses to discuss the issue, even to just meet with us. He says his back's against the corner. Sure wish we had his corner. I wonder if he'd consider hunger striking to promote his policy. Probably not, it's too hard. He just hides in his office.

The reporter turns back to the camera.

REPORTER:

Thank you, Eric. And now, back to the studio.

Cadieux is silent. The Spirit is standing near him, with arms folded and a self-satisfied smile on her face.

PRESENT:

Don't tell me they've hurt your feelings?

CADIEUX:

I'm really not a bad person, you know.

The Spirit studies him for a moment. The smile fades from her face.

PRESENT:

You know what the sad thing is? You're probably not. You're probably a family man who loves his wife and kids. You're just a poor misguided bureaucrat who seriously thinks he's doing the right thing. It would almost be better if you were an evil person. Too bad.

The Spirit shakes her head and turns toward her bundle of clothing on the floor. Cadieux, feeling miserable, runs toward her.

CADIEUX:

You're not leaving, are you?

PRESENT:

Got to go to a college graduation. Don't know how many more I'll be seeing in the future. What does it matter to you? I thought you didn't like me anyways.

CADIEUX:

Unsure why he stopped her.   I don't. I just don't know what to do now. Any suggestions?

PRESENT:

Oh don't give me a straight line like that. It's too tempting. But before I go, I'd like to show you something. You got any kids, Cadieux?

CADIEUX:

Yeah, two.

PRESENT:
They cute? Clean?

CADIEUX:
Insulted. Of course.

PRESENT:
Take a look at this.

She grabs the shawl and whips it off the bundle. Instead of clothes underneath, there are two dirty, wretched-looking children. They are shivering and quite miserable. Cadieux steps back.

CADIEUX:
My God, what are they?

PRESENT:
God had very little to do with them, me Bucko. These are man-made.

The children crawl toward the Spirit and huddle against her legs as she puts her shawl on.

PRESENT:
The girl is Want, the boy Ignorance. Beware of them, Cadieux, both of them, but especially the boy. For Ignorance can call Want, and the two can live as one.

CADIEUX:
What are they doing with you?

SPIRIT:
They huddle under my shawl of Understanding and come to me for warmth and protection.

They've been with me for a long time, Cadieux,
but some day I hope they'll be gone, that Ignorance
and Want will no longer hover around Education
Present. For you see, Mr. Cadieux, I really hate
being a working mother.

*And with a flourish she's gone, leaving Cadieux
alone. By this point, Cadieux is feeling pretty out
of it. Too much is happening at too fast a pace. He
sits down with a thud, somewhat dazed.*

CADIEUX:

There's no place like home, there's no place like
home.

*He is quiet for a moment, feeling despondent,
when a new realization dawns on him. It's almost
like he's caught his second wind.*

CADIEUX:

Wait a minute, why am I feeling guilty? Am I my
Indian's keeper? I refuse to feel guilty over all this.
I will not carry the burden of 500,000 Native
people on my back. Just because I'm the Minister
of Indian Affairs is no reason to blame me for
everything that goes wrong. *Starts yelling to the
world around him.* Do you think I like all this?
Almost pathetically. If it was up to me I'd let
everybody in Canada go to school free, really I
would. I'm only human, too. I had to do this to
keep my job. I never wanted this position anyways.
I'm huddled against the wind in Otter Lake while
Mulroney is working on his tan in Bangkok. I look
just as good in a bathing suit as he does.

Cadieux sits down again in a state of depression.
He rests his chin on his hands.

CADIEUX:
Where am I, anyways? One more Spirit to go, then
I'll be home free, I hope. *He sits there quietly for*
a moment, waiting. I wonder if these guys got
pagers or an answering service.

FUTURE/Guard:
Excuse me, do you have an appointment?

Cadieux is startled and almost has a heart attack
as he wheels around to see a security guard with a
clipboard. This is the Spirit of Education Future.
He keeps changing work clothes mysteriously
every few minutes, illustrating the possibilities
that the future can hold. Education Future is
looking at Cadieux inquisitively, waiting for an
answer.

CADIEUX:
Ahhh ...

They stand there looking at each other, the guard
calm, Cadieux holding his chest and breathing
hard.

CADIEUX:
Yelling. Why do you spirits always sneak up on
people from behind? You'd think you were a bunch
of Indians or something.

He realizes what he's said and puts his hand over
his mouth in a combination of fear and shame.
The guard calmly looks at his clipboard.

FUTURE/Guard:

Ah yes, you must be Mr. Ebenezer Cadieux, here to see the Spirit of Education Future. Excuse me, but is Cadieux spelt EUI or IEU?

CADIEUX:

Startled. IEU.

The guard rubs out something on his clipboard and corrects it, mumbling to himself.

FUTURE/Guard:

It's so hard to find good help these days, know what I mean? Of course you do, you're in the government. If you'll wait here, I'll notify the Spirit of Education Future.

Education Future as the security guard turns and leaves. Curious and timid, Cadieux follows a little bit but quickly loses him.

CADIEUX:

Hello, Mr. Guard. If this Education Future chap is busy, that's okay. You could just show me to the exit, that would be just as fine. Hello. *No response.* Damn!

FUTURE/Executive:

I believe we have an appointment.

The Spirit shows up from behind, scaring Cadieux again. Only this time the Spirit is wearing a three-piece suit and looking quite dapper. He has an air of wealth about him.

CADIEUX:

Angry and startled.   Will you people quit doing that?!?

FUTURE/Executive:

My apologies, old sport, that's the name of the game as we say in the business. So what can my company do for you, Mr. Cadieux?

CADIEUX:

Nothing, just get me out of here.

The executive shakes his head.

FUTURE/Executive:

I'm sorry but that just isn't feasible at the current time.

Cadieux seems to recognize the linguistic pattern of the Spirit.

CADIEUX:

Have you ever worked in government?

FUTURE/Executive:

Many times and in many ways, but that was a previous portfolio. So you're the famous Ebenezer Cadieux. You've become quite a legend, sir, here at the corporation anyways. But somehow I thought you'd be more ... imposing. Ah but that is the nature of legends, is it not, Mr. Cadieux?

CADIEUX:

I ... I guess so.

FUTURE/Executive:

Ah well, time is money and ours is running out.
Do you know why you're here, sir?

CADIEUX:

Well, if you're like all the rest of the Spirits, I guess
you are going to show me some incidents in the
future. Am I right?

FUTURE/Executive:

Very good, Mr. Cadieux. It's quite evident that you
didn't sleep your way to the top. *Looks at him
again.* Quite evident. Time for our first appointment. Observe.

*The Spirit waves his hand and they are in a band
office. In front of them are a young woman and an
older man. Both look concerned.*

WOMAN:

But there must be some way we can work this out.
There's gotta be.

MAN:

I wish there was, but what I've told you is the
truth. There's no money left to send you. You
know the priority: people already in school first;
people living on the reserve second; then other
band members. You've been living off-reserve for
five years now.

WOMAN:

But I'll move back after school, honest I will.

MAN:

That's not the point. There's just no money left.

WOMAN:

What am I going to do now? I was counting on DIA for tuition.

MAN:

Have you tried other government funding sources?

WOMAN:

Oh come on, you know they won't touch Native people. It's always the same answer, "You have your own source of funding, you're not our responsibility. Request denied." DIA won't fund me, nobody else will fund me. It's like I'm in an economic Bermuda triangle, where all sources of funding disappear.

MAN:

Why don't you try again next year, you may have a better chance.

WOMAN:

I doubt it. I'm already accepted in pre-med, I may not get in next year. And I doubt if the priorities will change. I've got to accept it, that's life.

MAN:

If it's any consolation, I had to turn down three other people last week. One was my cousin.

WOMAN:

Sorry, that's not much consolation. What will happen to me? I have to do something.

MAN:

Yesterday I saw a waitressing position available at the highway restaurant.

The woman looks crestfallen as what the man said sinks in. Mr. Cadieux turns to the Spirit, only to find him dressed in a white lab coat and glasses, resembling a doctor.

CADIEUX:

Surprised. What the ...

FUTURE/Doctor:

Not a pleasant concept, is it, Mr. Cadieux?

Cadieux is still trying to figure out the outfit change.

CADIEUX:

Um, no, I guess not ...

FUTURE/Doctor:

But that is a potential prognosis of the situation. Back in your time, the government ignored the symptoms of the disease, thinking it would clear up and go away. Like an infection it festered and spread until what you have just seen is a national ailment.

CADIEUX:

It's not my fault.

FUTURE/Doctor:

Everything starts somewhere, Mr. Cadieux. As one Native politician put it back in the 1990s, Cadieux is to ignorance what a woman named Mary was to typhoid.

CADIEUX:
> That's not fair!

FUTURE/Doctor:
> Get undressed. That young woman would have
> made a fine doctor. She could have found a cure for
> cancer, a disease you might get some day.

YOUNG WOMAN:
> Instead, I can expect to spend the rest of my life
> throwing hamburgers across a table.

FUTURE/Doctor:
> And as you said, Mr. Cadieux, that's not fair.

CADIEUX:
> So what do you want from me? Do you want me to
> reverse the decision? Is that what you want? If I
> promise that, will that get me out of this stupid
> place and back to where I belong?

FUTURE/Doctor:
> Sorry, it's not that easy. There are complications
> involved. Just reversing your decision would only
> mask the problem, you have to dig deeper, find the
> real reason why your infection must be halted.

CADIEUX:
> And just how do we do this?

FUTURE/Doctor:
> By making a house call. You let loose a snowball at
> the top of a hill. Now we will see what arrived at
> the bottom.

CADIEUX:

The only snow around here is in your head and it's melting. Every man has a limit and I've reached mine. Cough up, Doctor Spirit, where exactly is this house call?

FUTURE/Doctor:

A university in the far future, Mr. Cadieux, where many sciences are taught. But for tonight, political science is under the microscope. They are studying your policies, Mr. Cadieux.

CADIEUX:

Studying?

FUTURE/Doctor:

The 20th-century cap on post-secondary school education.

CADIEUX:

And I'll just bet the whole class is full of propaganda and you're full of something else. I demand to be properly represented in this class. If it's about the 20th-century aboriginal political structure, who better to teach that class than me? It's my reputation and my policies that are being examined.

The Spirit smiles a secret smile.

FUTURE/Doctor:

Very well. Proceed if you must.

Ebenezer Cadieux becomes a teacher in a futuristic university classroom. He is much more reserved and instructional. He uses a pointer during his lecture.

CADIEUX (as TEACHER):

You in the third row, what does COPSSE stand for?
Wake up. I look out at your shining little white
faces and I tremble for the future. COPSSE.
C.O.P.S.S.E. is an acronym meaning the Cap On
Post-Secondary School Education. Why? you ask.
Why would the government decide to limit the
amount of money available for Native students to
pursue a higher level of education? Was it because
it was becoming too expensive to finance the
growing number of students? Was it because the
then Minister of Indian Affairs was a certifiable
crackpot? Or was it really a political move aimed
at restricting the call for Native self-government?
Think about it. We know the Native people fought
COPSSE tooth and nail. Marches, hunger strikes,
plays were written about it. Several years later
Cadieux was almost assassinated by Cree terror-
ists. Lucky for him his policy made it impossible
for them to properly put their bomb together.
Couldn't read the instructions. At any rate,
COPSSE was passed. Native enrollment in post-
secondary schools went down. It's all there in your
textbook under "The Cadieux Tragedy." Now, if
you will turn to holographic plate number 14, we'll
examine something very interesting. *He stops
and looks at a student.* Young man, remove the
plate from your book and place it in the slot at the
top of your desk. *Impatiently.* You've got it in
backwards. *Waits.* Yes, very good indeed.

*Three visions of Native people in a possible future
where COPSSE is law appear, like holographs.*

CADIEUX:

Now here we have three versions of the current aboriginal life. Ah yes. You may already be familiar with this example.

Cadieux points to a dirty-looking Indian who looks as if he was born on the streets and has been walked on ever since.

What we have here is a specimen known by many names: bum, tramp, alcoholic, national disgrace. Their numbers have grown extensively over the last 100 years. Because of their limited and often inferior education, they seem unable to interface with our increasingly technological world. They leave reserves hoping to find improvement, but usually only to find disillusionment. A truly sad case. Next we have the most common sector of Native society, the Reserve Indian.

He points to a young man in worn jeans and soiled windbreaker, huddled against the wind.

The majority of the Native population has re-treated to their traditional lands, called reserves. Unable or unwilling to face the complicated world outside, they've developed a siege mentality, a growing sense of paranoia and resentment. The population continues to rise, but the available land does not. Reserves today are seriously overpopu-lated by neurotic and socially dysfunctional people. Again. Quite sad.

Cadieux points to a young woman, standing tall, and nicely dressed. She would almost be white if not for her skin color.

And finally, we have the Integrator. She looks okay by our standards, eh? Better than the other two, huh? In some ways. She is wealthier, more comfortable in the white world, and very vertically mobile. She helped design the holographic plates we're watching. She's also an outcast. She started out telling people she was Spanish or Hawaiian. Now she has everything she wants. Except her people. Saddest of all, I think. You'd think there would be a middle ground in all of this. You'd like to believe there are other alternatives. Cadieux, in his infinite naiveté, certainly thought so. But oddly, he wasn't around long enough to witness the effects of his actions.

Cadieux realizes what he has just said and reacts.

CADIEUX:
What do you mean, I wasn't around long enough to witness the effect of my actions? What happened to me?

INTEGRATOR:
No one is really sure.

RESERVE:
All we have today is a legend.

STREET INDIAN:
One dark and cold winter, Mr. Cadieux went into the bush ...

INTEGRATOR:
... to a very distant ...

RESERVE:

... remote ...

STREET INDIAN:

... northern Indian reserve. Ever since that fateful trip rumors have run crazy and wild.

CHORUS:

Rumors ...

STREET INDIAN:

... of a simple walk taken by Mr. Cadieux down by the frozen lake where something even colder than the ice he walked on was waiting for him. Cree and Ojibway legends tell of a spirit wandering those forests, a spirit called ... the Windigo! ... A spirit so cold and harsh it doesn't even like itself. The Windigo wanders the woods looking for people to possess.

RESERVE:

Cadieux was possessed.

STREET INDIAN:

Or so they say.

INTEGRATOR:

But what do the people up there know? They just simple Indians.

STREET INDIAN:

To this very day, people still talk about a crazy old man wandering the forests and muskeg of the north ...

STREET INDIAN:

> ... his body wracked by a hunger that won't go away ...

RESERVE:

> ... gobbling up students ...

INTEGRATOR:

> ... wherever he can find them.

STREET INDIAN:

> But it's just a story.

CHORUS:

> We think.

> *Cadieux turns away from the scene with a scream of agony.*

CADIEUX:

> Enough, Spirit, I've heard enough!

> *He finds the Spirit dressed in work-pants, a lumber-jacket and a hard-hat. To his left is the Spirit of Education Past; to his right, the Spirit of Education Present.*

CADIEUX:

> Oh Spirit, tell me it won't be this way. Tell me there's another way.

FUTURE/Worker:

> Beats me.

CADIEUX:

What do you mean, "beats me?" You're the Spirit of Education Future, you're supposed to know everything!

FUTURE/Worker:

I only know what can be, not what will be, a small but important difference. Everybody chooses their own future, Mr. Cadieux. I just help build 'em, I don't design 'em.

CADIEUX:

You mean I might not end up eating students in Otter Lake?

PAST:

I hope not. I got friends up there.

Cadieux steps back, not knowing how to take all three Spirits.

CADIEUX:

Hey, this is not fair, three against one.

PRESENT:

Actually, it's about 500,000 against one. I hope you can run good.

FUTURE:

You have seen a lot in the last little while, but have you seen enough?

CADIEUX:

Okay, okay, maybe I was a little reckless with my decision. But it's still not too late to change. I can go back and change things, can't I?

FUTURE:

All things are possible.

CADIEUX:

So what happens now?

PAST:

We give you knowledge, now you give us something.

CADIEUX:

What?

FUTURE:

A promise. To reexamine COPSSE.

Mr. Cadieux, released by the Spirits, straightens his tie.

CADIEUX:

Well, I can's make any promises at this point. It's up to the people of Canada to decide the policy of the country, not just a few. But I will take it under consideration, trust me.

PRESENT:

But you promised!

CADIEUX:

Did I? I was merely under a lot of pressure. This hasn't exactly been a walk through the park, you know.

PAST:

Me knew promise no good.

PRESENT:
>   You no-good scum-sucking son of a ...

Education Future interrupts her quickly.

FUTURE:
>   After all we've shown you, that is all you have to
>   say?

CADIEUX:
>   That's politics.

PRESENT:
>   There are a lot of people out there, both Native and
>   non-Native, who won't accept this.

CADIEUX:
>   Again, that's politics. When I'm shown the major-
>   ity of Canadians don't agree with it, then I'll talk.
>   Until then, the show is over.

*Cadieux picks up his briefcase and walks smartly
down the center aisle, leaving the three Spirits of
Education standing with their mouths gaping.*

THE END

Photo courtesy: Tom King

Drew Hayden Taylor, prolific and award-winning Ojibway writer from Curve Lake in Central Ontario, is a jack-of-all-trades and truly the master of one – playwriting. With a universally appealing repertoire ranging from imaginative plays for young audiences to witty comedies as well as poignant dramas, he has most certainly earned the right to be hailed as "one of Canada's leading Native playwrights." In fact, Drew likes to say that he is "married to theatre but has many mistresses" – to whom he is obviously equally devoted, judging from the success of his various short stories, novels, screenplays, and essays. His most recent literary endeavours include the novel and finalist in the Governor General's Literary Awards, *Motorcycles & Sweetgrass* (2010); a collection of essays, *News – Postcards from the Four Directions* (2011); and a comedy, *Dead White Writer on the Floor* (2011). Whether Drew is spicing up life on the reserve with a contemporary tale of the trickster, presenting us with a smorgasbord of his adventures abroad and at home, or allowing six stereotyped Indians to re-concoct their identities, it all boils downs to doing what he does best – storytelling. For "stories are memories that must be shared with the Universe because if they aren't, the Universe becomes a much smaller place." (*Toronto at Dreamers Rock*)